═══ ONE TO ONE ═══
Interviewing, Selecting, Appraising, and Counseling Employees

James G. Goodale

Philbrook, Goodale Associates
Houston, Texas

PRENTICE HALL
Englewood Cliffs, New Jersey 07632

Prentice-Hall International (UK) Limited, *London*
Prentice-Hall of Australia Pty. Limited, *Sydney*
Prentice-Hall Canada, Inc., *Toronto*
Prentice-Hall Hispanoamericana, S.A., *Mexico*
Prentice-Hall of India Private Limited, *New Delhi*
Prentice-Hall of Japan, Inc., *Tokyo*
Simon & Schuster Asia Pte. Ltd., *Singapore*
Editora Prentice-Hall do Brasil, Ltda., *Rio de Janeiro*

10 9 8 7 6 5 4 3 2 1

Portions of this book were previously
published as *The Fine Art of Interviewing*.

Library of Congress Cataloging-in-Publication Data

Goodale, James G.
    One to one : interviewing, selecting, appraising, and counseling
employees / James G. Goodale.
        p.   cm.
    Includes bibliographical references and index.
    ISBN 0-13-553256-6
    1. Employment interviewing. 2. Employee selection.
    3. Employees—Rating of. 4. Employee counseling. I. Title.
HF5549.5.I6G623   1992
658.3'1--dc20   91-45455
                                                           CIP

ISBN 0-13-553256-6

PRENTICE HALL
Professional Publishing
Englewood Cliffs, NJ 07632
Simon & Schuster. A Paramount Communications Company

Printed in the United States of America

TO ROBIN

Preface

This is a book about how to plan and conduct effective and lawful business interviews. If you are a supervisor, manager, project leader, team member, recruiter, or human resource specialist, or aspiring to these positions, you will find the book helpful. It is broader in scope than most interviewing books, which typically cover only one type of interview. The book contains five key interviews commonly conducted in the business world—selection, performance appraisal, counseling, career planning, and disciplinary.

Although the book draws on a broad body of research and knowledge from business management and applied psychology, the material it contains can be readily applied. The book offers a clear, practical approach that guides you to the two essential ingredients of every effective interview—the content to include and the techniques to cover that content. The book also presents legislation relevant to each interview and specific guidance for how to avoid legal problems.

The book's unique strength is its flexibility. When each type of interview is presented, there is no script for you to follow or long lists of questions for you to ask. No magic script or set of questions exists from which you can create the perfect interview. Rather, the book presents an approach to planning and conducting interviews, with specific guidelines and steps for you to follow. The goal is to provide guidance but still allow you the flexibility to adjust to the situation, the person you are interviewing, and your own personal style. These guidelines show you how to formulate the job-related, legal topics to include in your own interviews. The book also includes a large number of techniques for you to use in conducting effective interviews. Finally, each chapter emphasizes two-way communication and is packed with examples of how to draw information from the interviewee in a conversational way.

The information in the book is unique; I have developed and refined it over the past 20 years. The material has proven effective in hundreds of training courses attended by supervisors, managers, recruiters, and human resource specialists. The response of thousands of working people to the training courses has been universally positive. They find the material clear, logical, practical, and effective.

The book is especially timely today. Continuing emphasis on quality, recent increases in the cost of employee benefits and salaries, and the decreasing supply of applicants for entry-level jobs have placed increased pressure on all employers to hire and retain high-quality employees. In addition, well-educated, career-oriented job applicants expect much from their employers. In particular, they expect to participate in a fair, job-related selection interview with each prospective employer. Once hired, they expect their immediate supervisors to take an active part in developing their careers through regular feedback about the quality of their performance and discussions about their job-related problems and career plans. Unfortunately, most supervisors and managers still learn how to deal with employees through trial and error and need clear, practical guidance in how to improve their relationships with employees through the interviews covered in the book.

In addition to specific guidelines and techniques, the book includes three topics of great concern to anyone who conducts interviews in today's business world. The first is the growing emphasis on teamwork. As employers share power with employees through participative management and self-managed work teams, many employees are responsible for decisions previously reserved for managers and supervisors. For example, team members interview job applicants and make hiring recommendations. In growing numbers of project teams, employees evaluate the performance of their peers and even their project leaders. Furthermore, co-workers are often more effective than supervisors or managers in employee counseling and career planning because they can identify more strongly with the employees seeking guidance. This book's emphasis on two-way communication provides specific guidelines to help non-supervisory employees conduct effective interviews without relying on formal authority.

The second topic of concern is the impact of Equal Employment Opportunity legislation on the legality of decisions made in interviews. Personal characteristics of interviewees and the personal preferences and biases of interviewers can strongly influence the perceptions, judgments, and outcomes of interviews. Unskillful interviewers may find themselves and their employers open to charges of discrimination. I have reviewed all relevant legislation and have included specific guidelines to minimize your liability under this legislation.

The third is game playing by well trained and rehearsed interviewees. Especially in selection interviews, we have entered the age of the professional interviewee with prepared answers and a practiced style that prevent inexperienced interviewers from obtaining needed information. The book shows exactly how you can cut through the game playing and draw out the real person in the interview.

Many people have contributed to the ideas in the book. Ron Burke and Tim Hall, my former academic colleagues, influenced me as I began developing my approach to interviewing, and Tom Philbrook, my business partner, has provided valuable counsel and encouragement. I also owe much to the Society for Human Resource Management, the College Placement Council, and the Human Resources Professionals Association of Ontario for providing me the opportunity to reach their members through seminars and presentations. I want to thank my clients from the human resource, training, and recruiting departments of hundreds of corporations for whom I have conducted interviewing training courses over the years. My greatest debt, however, is to the thousands of supervisors, managers, recruiters, and human resource specialists who have attended my training courses and put my ideas into practice. In working with them I have tested and refined much of the material included in the book.

I also want to thank Prentice Hall for its support in publishing the book. Jeff Krames, Paul Becker, John Willig, Philip Ruppel, and Sybil Grace have provided encouragement and guidance over the past few years.

Finally, I want to thank my wife, Robin, to whom the book is dedicated. A fine writer and editor in her own right, she has encouraged me throughout the writing of the book. She has read the entire manuscript and has made excellent editorial suggestions to assist me in presenting my ideas clearly and succinctly.

James G. Goodale

Introduction

Imagine yourself in any of the following situations:

- As a recently promoted new supervisor, you have a vacancy to fill in your department. The human resource department has advertised for the position and sent you the résumés of ten well-qualified applicants. You are to review the résumés, interview the applicants you are interested in, and make the final selection decision. You try not to panic, but you have only a vague idea of what to do next and how to conduct the interviews.
- One of your most consistent performers has come in to work at least 30 minutes late three times during the past two weeks and has missed the deadline on an important project. When you drop by her office to speak to her about it, she closes the door, bursts into tears, and says that her marriage is falling apart. You're at a loss for words.
- As a department head with 15 years of supervisory experience, you have never received a formal assessment of your performance or discussed your career with your boss, nor have you formally discussed job performance and careers with your staff. Your company has always relied on day-to-day feedback, operating on the principle of "no news is good news." However, the corporation that recently acquired your small firm has comprehensive programs for performance appraisal and career development, and you are expected to conduct such interviews and discussions with each member of your staff within the next quarter.
- The special project team you joined after graduation late last year

has just begun its semi-annual meeting on team performance appraisal. As the junior member of the nine-person team, you have looked forward to this opportunity to learn more about what your co-workers and project leader think of your performance to date. The team's method of performance appraisal surprises you, however. Not only will each team member meet with you to discuss your performance, but you are expected to meet with each member to discuss his or her performance, including the project leader who has 25 years of experience in your field. You have no idea about how to approach these meetings.

- During your five years in supervision, you have been fortunate enough not to have any "problem employees" although you have heard several other supervisors complain about employees who bend the rules or perform poorly. Three months ago, however, you were promoted into another department, and you inherited a real problem—a veteran employee who barely meets minimal performance standards and stretches his lunch breaks. Today he took a day off without your permission, and you stormed down to the human resource department to report the unauthorized absence and to request that he be disciplined. The human resource manager told you to read the Progressive Discipline section of your supervisory handbook thoroughly, come to her for any guidance, and give the employee a verbal warning when he returns to work. You're dreading the meeting.

Sound familiar? If so, you're not alone. Every supervisor and manager is expected to conduct interviews routinely. There are selection interviews to be held with job applicants, and performance appraisal, counseling, career planning, and disciplinary interviews to be held with current employees. In addition, many non-supervisory employees conduct selection interviews with job applicants, and performance appraisal, counseling, and career planning interviews with members of their project team or department. But highly skilled interviewers are surprisingly rare because most people receive very little guidance in how to interview. This book will show you how to design and conduct effective interviews.

LEARNING HOW TO INTERVIEW

It is a pleasure to watch an effective interviewer who relaxes the other person by striking up an almost immediate rapport, conducts a smooth, seemingly effortless and unstructured conversation, and then ends the interview only after having covered all necessary topics and having collected all needed information. Many of us have known people who appear to conduct effective interviews almost by intuition and seem to have the knack of saying the right thing at the right time. We are inclined to attribute their success to personality and intuitive feel and therefore conclude that a good interviewer is born, not made.

This conclusion, however, is simply not true.

There is much that we do *not* see as we watch an effective interviewer. You can be sure that training in basic principles, hours of study and practice, and careful planning have preceded the finished product. We are familiar with many types of performance that appear effortless but are grounded in years of training and practice. Just as the professional athlete, the ballet dancer, and the professional comedian have planned and practiced each individual action we observe in their seemingly effortless performance, effective interviewers have worked very hard to perfect their techniques. As with any other highly skilled performance, interviewing must be grounded in sound principles and excellent technique.

Effective interviewing can be systematically learned as a highly developed management skill. Unfortunately, people are often expected to learn how to interview through a process of osmosis. Typically, people in supervisory positions are expected to bring a high level of interviewing skill to their jobs (the skill somehow automatically comes with the job title), but most learn how to interview through trial and error.

The same is true of people who work in human resource or personnel departments and are therefore called upon to conduct selection, career planning, and counseling interviews. Many supervisors and managers assume that these people are experts in interviewing and look to them for guidance. In fact, their training often consists of sitting in with another, more experienced employee during a couple of interview sessions and then being turned loose on their own. As many of you may have already discovered, this trial-and-error learning can be as frightening and painful as it is ineffective.

THE IMPORTANCE OF EFFECTIVE INTERVIEWS

Interviewing is one of every manager's most important responsibilities because effectiveness in conducting interviews strongly influences the success of both the manager and his or her staff. Furthermore, poor interviews can cost employers millions of dollars in recruiting and training expenses, lost productivity, and lawsuits. Managers routinely select new employees, evaluate their performance and help them plan their careers, and counsel or discipline employees who perform poorly. All these responsibilities are carried out in interviews.

Every working person is significantly affected by interviews throughout his or her association with an employer. The association begins with a **selection interview**, the most common and important of this book's five interviews. The interview is the most highly trusted and widely used device to help an employer choose the best person for the job. Selection decisions represent not only a major financial investment by an employer, but also a major personal investment by an individual. The decision of both parties is strongly influenced by the interview. Unfortunately, the typical selection interview suffers from many weaknesses, pitfalls, and potential legal liabilities. Chapter 2 discusses these problems and provides specific guidance for designing and conducting legal, effective selection interviews.

After several months on the job, the new employee is likely to take part in a variety of additional interviews. Most managers conduct some form of **performance appraisal interview** with their employees at least once a year. This is the interview that nearly all business people have experienced and many dislike. In this interview, the employee's past performance is reviewed and evaluated, and plans are made to help the employee reach performance goals in the future. Salary increases and promotions may also be discussed in performance appraisal interviews, and these topics add to the importance of the interview to both the manager and the employee. Many supervisors and managers feel uncomfortable evaluating the performance of their employees. Chapter 3 will show you how to avoid judging others and making them defensive when conducting performance appraisal interviews. You will learn how to draw out employees' assessments of their own performance and encourage them to set their own work goals and developmental plans.

Many managers also participate in counseling interviews and disciplinary interviews. Both require a great deal of skill because they are held with employees who need help. These interviews can be highly emotional and very difficult discussions for both parties. **Counseling interviews** often catch the interviewer unprepared because employees usually initiate these interviews when they are experiencing stress from a personal or work-related problem that interferes with their job performance. Chapter 4 gives you specific steps to coach and counsel employees and help them understand and solve their own problems.

Some managers also conduct **career planning interviews,** in which employees identify the types of jobs they wish to pursue in the organization and set plans to help them achieve these career goals through training and work assignments. This interview is clearly of critical importance to the success of both the manager and his or her staff, although it is too often overlooked in today's organizations. Chapter 5 gives you detailed guidance that will help you focus on your employees' careers to reduce turnover and enhance job performance and satisfaction.

Chapter 6 deals with **disciplinary interviews,** the interview that people fear the most. Managers initiate the disciplinary interview, a confrontational discussion with an employee who has violated an important rule or policy or who has consistently performed below acceptable standards. You will learn how this interview fits into a formal, legal system of progressive discipline. The chapter also includes specific do's and don'ts and shows you how to plan and conduct disciplinary interviews that are truly *corrective,* rather than punitive.

All these interviews conducted by managers, supervisors, project leaders, team members, or human resource specialists are of major importance to the organization's objective of placing and keeping the right people in the right jobs. These interviews strongly influence the job performance and work satisfaction of the typical employee and are therefore crucial to *your* success. Whatever job you currently hold, this book will help you improve your interviewing skills.

James G. Goodale

Contents

5. CAREER PLANNING INTERVIEW • 153

6. DISCIPLINARY INTERVIEWING • 185

ENDNOTES • 209

INDEX • 217

The Keys to Effective Interviews

1

Many important business transactions take place in interviews. These transactions contribute significantly to the success of each employee and the organization as a whole. Interviews that are poorly conceived and conducted, however, can have negative effects on both the employer and the employee. Let's begin by examining the major risks of poor interviews and then discussing in detail how you can avoid these problems by planning and conducting effective interviews.

CONSEQUENCES OF POOR INTERVIEWING

Interviewing is a highly subjective process. There is a disturbing amount of evidence to indicate that, if two members of an organization interview the same person at different times, the outcome

1

of the interviews will differ. For example, if two managers interview the same job applicant, one may recommend hiring the applicant, but the other may not be at all impressed with the person. Similarly, if a troubled employee goes to two different people for counseling, he or she might leave one interview feeling misunderstood and intimidated, while the other interview might lead to excellent problem-solving and a viable plan for improvement. Of course, interviewers will almost invariably differ somewhat in their styles and in the way they interpret information and make decisions. More than a small degree of inconsistency, however, can create serious problems for an organization.

There are three major problems that result from poor interviewing. They are:

1. Failure to meet interview objectives

2. Poor public relations and employee relations

3. Charges of discrimination

Let's deal with each in turn.

Failure to meet interview objectives. An interview is an important business transaction designed to meet specific objectives. If interviewers do not identify the objectives and systematically set out to accomplish them, the interview will likely fail. For example, the wrong applicant may be selected for the job, the employee's training needs will not be identified and discussed in a performance appraisal interview, or the lack of promotional opportunities in a department will not be uncovered in a series of career planning interviews. All these failures waste time and money.

Poor public relations and employee relations. As serious as failure to meet objectives is, it may be the least of the poor interviewer's worries. We must consider the interviewee's perception of a poor interview. Untrained or unskilled interviewers are perceived by employees or job applicants as incompetent, arbitrary, or unfair. Applicants who are subjected to amateurish selection interviews with canned psychological questions ("If you could control what people say about you, what would you want them to say," or "What are your strengths, ... weaknesses?") or questionable tactics (like interrupting and insulting applicants presumably to measure reaction to stress) form low opinions of the organization doing the hiring. This adds up to a poor image and poor public relations for the organization. Managers who have bungled performance appraisal, counseling, or career planning interviews with their own employees know the costs. Nothing can destroy a supervisor-employee relationship more quickly than an interview on crucial matters (promotion potential, future with the company, nagging work problem) conducted by a seemingly uncaring or unfair boss.

Charges of discrimination. Poor interviewers also run the risk of having their organizations sued for discrimination. Untrained interviewers often base their decisions to hire, promote, or discipline someone on their own intuition or the other person's personality. Such highly subjective judgments may violate local, state, or federal laws and are therefore open to the challenge of being discriminatory. To avoid such challenges, interviewers need to understand what practices are allowed and prohibited by a large number of federal laws and Supreme Court decisions, from the Civil Rights Act of 1964 to the Americans with Disabilities Act of 1990 and the Civil Rights Act of 1991. In addition, societal issues such as homosexual lifestyle, increased employee turnover due to employees' escalating concerns with their own career development and a drop in the loyalty of employers, and the AIDS epidemic have placed additional responsibility on organizations to avoid practices that appear to discriminate against certain groups of employees or job applicants.

The potential for discrimination is particularly great in selection interviewing. Title VII of the Civil Rights Act of 1964 prohibits discrimination in employment because of race, color, religion, sex, or national origin. This original legislation and a number of more recent laws, executive orders, and court cases provide two clear warnings to employers. First, make sure your selection interviewers base their hiring decisions on job-related information.

Second, if you are challenged in court, be able to demonstrate that selection interviews actually predict how well individuals will perform on the job. Under close scrutiny, many organizations might fail to meet these two criteria.

The possibility of charges of discrimination extends beyond the selection interview. Title VII of the Civil Rights Act also requires employers to keep for six months records pertinent to hiring, promotion, demotion, transfer, layoff or termination, and rates of pay of employees. Disciplinary, performance appraisal, counseling, and career planning interviews frequently contribute to decisions on all these matters. These interviews must be done carefully so that decisions are made on the basis of job-related information. If the interviewer can be accused of firing or failing to promote an employee because of differences in lifestyle, a "personality conflict," intuition, or fear of AIDS, the organization may be open to the charge of discrimination.

On a positive note, nothing in all these laws and court decisions interferes fundamentally with sensible, effective management policies and practices. They do require, however, that all employers take care in establishing and carrying out those policies and practices. Suffice it to say that skillful interviewers can help the organization to avoid major problems.

GAME PLAYING IN THE INTERVIEW

Interviews have always included an element of game playing in which each party tries to outfox the other. Many people try to guess what the interviewer is looking for and then give the interviewer only that part of the information that is to their own advantage, while hiding their weaknesses. For example, in a performance appraisal interview, the employee asked for a self-evaluation may emphasize the strengths of last year's job performance and downplay the blunders. Meanwhile, the intrepid interviewer tries to break through the respondent's facade, often using trick questions or other devious techniques, to get a look at the real person. As a result, the interview may degenerate into a game in which each party tries to outguess and trick the other. On the other hand, people who do not "play the game" and are more open and honest in interviews or even understate their accomplishments may be at a disadvantage.

It appears that such game playing is more common in interviews today than it was 20 or 25 years ago. A major reason for this trend is that interviewees are receiving more guidance and are growing more skillful. We have definitely entered the age of the professional interviewee. While this is true for all interviews covered in this book, it is especially well illustrated in the selection interview. Anyone who has interviewed recent university graduates applying for a job has probably encountered the well-prepared, smooth applicant who attempts to take control of a selection interview and run it to his or her own advantage. Of course, some applicants are still poorly prepared, but the trend appears to be toward a greater level of sophistication. Many applicants present laser-printed résumés, sometimes prepared with the help of a résumé-writing consultant. It is common for students to receive coaching and to participate in practice sessions for recruiting interviews. There are even seminars given on how to sell oneself in an interview. In addition, students often attend on-campus interviews just for practice. And several books[1] give sample questions for applicants to expect in selection interviews, and then suggest good answers. In general, people being interviewed are more sophisticated today than ever before.

However, supervisors and managers as well as non-supervisory employees and human resource specialists who conduct various kinds of interviews have not increased their skill over the past two decades. Newly hired employees are reporting the same blunders made by interviewers today that they reported 20 years ago. In

---

[1] Footnotes to chapters can be found at the back of the book in the section entitled Endnotes on page 209.

my two decades of conducting interviewing workshops, I have seen little change in the kinds of problems discussed by participants as they enter the course or their level of skill in interviewing. I believe this lack of expertise is due to the common business practice of assuming that people whose jobs involve communication can interview effectively with no additional training. As I have already mentioned, interviewing is difficult, highly skilled work that is seldom mastered through trial and error. I have seen game playing dramatically reduced as interviewers become more proficient. Skillful interviewers can cut quite quickly through the facade and tricks of a respondent, take control, and conduct effective and efficient interviews.

THE FUNDAMENTALS OF INTERVIEWING

Interviewing is a skill that can be learned. There are two essential ingredients of a successful interview: *content* and *conducting*. Content refers to the topics and questions included in the interview. Conducting refers to the way in which the interviewer covers content (e.g., relaxing respondents and getting them to volunteer needed information, phrasing questions and probing for additional information, knowing when to listen and when to speak, and guiding the conversation subtly). Interviewers must cover the appropriate topics and ask the right questions (content) to be successful. In addition, they must conduct the interview properly by using a variety of communication skills to open up the respondent and draw out the information being sought.

If either ingredient is lacking, the interviewer will fail. For example, some recruiters conduct selection interviews very smoothly, establishing rapport and probing deftly while maintaining an easy conversational tone, but they unfortunately ask irrelevant and unlawful questions and cover the wrong topics, so they are unable to evaluate the applicant's potential to perform the job. This is often the downfall of managers, supervisors, project leaders, and team members who communicate well but have little experience in systematically preparing the content of an interview.

Other people may plan the interview very carefully, listing topics and even questions to be covered, but they conduct the interview poorly. They fail to establish rapport, or they ask questions in a stilted, mechanical way that unsettles respondents and does not allow them to relax and open up. In this case, the interview may degenerate to the point that it sounds like an interrogation based on an orally administered questionnaire.

Content

Many interviews are weak in content. Most interviewers are more likely to fail because of poor content than because of their weakness in conducting the interview. This is true because people do not take the time or have the knowledge necessary to plan an interview systematically.

Each type of interview has several objectives; to design an effective interview, you must first know the objectives to be achieved. Next, you must consider the general approach and style of the interview. Should it be relaxed and conversational, or should it be more formal? The formality of the interview depends largely on objectives. For example, an informal style is desirable in a selection interview, but not in a disciplinary interview. Should the interview be highly structured with a long list of questions to be asked, or should it have no structure at all, allowing the interviewer the freedom of investigating any topic that seems relevant? I argue that the most effective interview is *semistructured;* that is, topics have been identified, but there is flexibility for you to adjust to the other person and use various communication skills and techniques to cover the topics as you wish.

Next, a format, or agenda, must be considered. Many interviewers waste time by repeating themselves and drifting off topic. A format that coincides with interview objectives will promote efficiency. The final step in planning an interview is to make a list of topics and in some cases a few questions to be covered

Table 1.1
SEQUENCE FOR PLANNING INTERVIEW CONTENT

Developmental Sequence	Illustration
I. Type of Interview	Selection Interview
II. Objectives	A. Collect information to assess
	1. Potential to perform the job
	2. Willingness to perform
	B. Provide information about the company, department, and job
	C. Check personal chemistry
III. Approach and style	A. Semistructured
	B. Tailored to the specific job
	C. Consistent
	D. Flexible and conversational
IV. Format	A. Establish rapport
	B. Set the agenda
	C. Collect information
	D. Provide information
	E. Invite applicant's questions
	F. Terminate the interview
V. Topics	A. Previous related work experience
	B. Previous training and education
	C. Hints of work interest and career plans
	D. Information about the company

faithfully during the interview. In summary, if you work through your format and cover a list of topics in the style you have chosen, then you will achieve your objectives, and the interview will be successful.

Many people faced with the chore of conducting an interview fail to plan its content properly because they do not work systematically through this sequence. Instead, they jump from Step I to Step V as outlined in Table 1.1. "Well," they say, "I have to see those applicants for the administrative assistant job. What shall I ask them?" or "I've got to do a performance appraisal interview with Jones next week. What can I say about her performance?"

Systematic planning for every interview is essential, but a well planned interview need not be rigid or awkward. In fact, a carefully planned and well conducted interview should appear to the respondent to have very little structure. The key here is flexibility. A semistructured approach allows needed flexibility for you to vary questioning techniques, phrasing, and style. This flexibility will allow you the freedom to make the interview appear like a smooth, unstructured conversation. This type of interview is quite rare and requires a high degree of skill.

Conducting

This brings us to the communication skills and techniques needed to transform a carefully planned, semistructured interview into an apparently unplanned, unstructured conversation. This is truly a management skill that can only be developed through practice. Like any other skill, conducting an interview is based on fundamentals which, if learned and practiced, will lead to success.

These fundamentals, outlined in Table 1.2, will be present in all five types of interviews discussed in this book. They will be clearer as I apply them to each specific type of interview, but it is useful to describe them in general terms now. Let's take them in order.

Table 1.2
TECHNIQUES FOR CONDUCTING INTERVIEWS

Sequence		Illustration
I. Initiate	State the purpose of the interview and get the interviewee talking	Open-ended questions
II. Listen	Listen actively and store topics to be pursued	Listen for your agenda items
III. Focus	Direct the interviewee's attention to topics raised that you want to probe	"You mentioned..." "I'm particularly interested in..."
IV. Probe	Probe into relevant topics raised by the interviewee and pursue additional topics you planned to cover	Specific questions like how, why, and results Non-directive techniques
V. Use	Use the information you have gained during the interview to meet your objectives	Conclude the interview appropriately, incorporating one or more of following: evaluations, decisions, and plans

Initiate. It's your interview, and you have the responsibility of establishing and maintaining control from the beginning. It is helpful to begin by summarizing the purpose of the interview. Then move into the body of the interview by asking open-ended questions. An example of such a question in a selection interview is, "I noticed on your résumé that your most recent job was in sales. What were your major responsibilities in that job?" In a performance appraisal interview, you might begin by asking, "How would you rate your performance in the past six months?" The objective here is to get the respondent talking about topics that *you* want to address in the interview.

Listen. I cannot overemphasize the importance of active listening in an interview. Many interviewers do not listen well because they are thinking up their next question while the respondent is talking, or they are feeling anxious because they don't know what to ask next. You can overcome these obstacles by careful preparation and good probing techniques during the interview. If you have prepared a list of topics you want to cover in the interview, active listening is simply hearing and remembering important subjects that you wish to pursue later. If you ask the right open-ended questions, the respondent will raise many of the topics on your prepared list.

Focus. In the interview you wish to cover your topics as efficiently as possible. It is therefore your responsibility to direct the respondent's attention to what you want to talk about. To do so, refer to something the respondent has already said and then begin probing further. For example, you might say, "You mentioned that your job involved maintaining good relationships with customers. How did you approach that part of your job?" Another example is, "You said you would rate your performance as excellent. What aspects of your performance were you particularly satisfied with these past six months?" These comments and questions not only focus the discussion, but they also add to the conversational tone of the interview. The purpose of initiating the interview with open-ended questions is to get respondents to raise some of *your* topics. Then when you follow up on their (your) topics, the interview appears more like an unplanned, unstructured conversation.

Probe. You need to probe and pry (in a friendly and professional manner) into what the respondent says until you learn what you are seeking in the interview. Many interviewers fail because they accept the first answer and then realize after the interview that they did not learn enough. This is the time to probe thoroughly the topics raised by the respondent, and then introduce and probe into additional topics you wish to cover.

Use. Every interview has a purpose beyond information gathering. The information must be used to evaluate, plan, and make decisions. In a selection interview, you must evaluate the applicant's potential and willingness to perform the job. In a counseling interview, problem definition should be followed by problem solving and goal setting. In an appraisal interview, the employee and supervisor may jointly assess the employee's past performance and make mutual plans for changes in the future. Having the information's use in mind during the interview not only helps you focus and probe effectively, but also helps you make use of the information during or shortly after the interview. You have not completed your responsibility as an interviewer until you have converted the raw information collected during the interview into the appropriate evaluation, plan, or decision.

INTERVIEWING SKILLS AND TECHNIQUES

Throughout the interview it is imperative that the interviewer keep the channels of communication wide open. A number of techniques promote maximum information flow between the two parties by encouraging the respondent to open up and talk in a relatively unguarded way. These techniques also help promote a smooth, conversational tone.

The key to effective interviewing is *flexibility.* These techniques provide guidance but still allow you the flexibility to adjust to the situation, the person being interviewed, and your own personal style. These techniques can be identified and practiced, but they cannot be programmed. They are alternatives available to interviewers, but you are not required to use all of them. Only experience will help you develop the skill in choosing among them—of knowing when to ask a specific question, when to nod your head, when to reflect a feeling, and when to say nothing.

Please note that overreliance on any of the techniques is ineffective. You need to draw from a wide range of responses and use each only as it seems to fit the situation.

Directive Techniques

1. *Open ended question.* An open-ended question is simply one that cannot be answered yes or no. While these questions are useful throughout the interview, they are particularly appropriate to *initiate* the discussion and encourage the respondent to talk. In a selection interview, an early open-ended question might be, "What were your major responsibilities in that job?" A career planning interview might include an early question such as, "What do you particularly like about your current job?"

2. *Specific probe.* Most interviewers do not probe enough, and therefore do not learn enough. This type of question is crucial to any interview's success because it draws additional information from interviewees. Specific probes vary depending on the type of interview, but they fall into the following four categories.

a. HOW?—What steps did you take? What was involved? What approach? What techniques? This type of probe uncovers the respondent's *work method.* For example,

RESPONDENT: "I've always had the ability to get my employees to extend themselves and work hard for me."

INTERVIEWER: "So you feel you've had success at motivating people. What specific steps do you take to get your employees to work hard for you?"

b. WHY?—What was your rationale? Why did you choose that method? This type of probe uncovers the *cause* of the respondent's work method.

c. HOW WELL?—What results did you achieve? How did your employees respond? What feedback did you receive? This type of probe uncovers the *results* of the respondent's work method.

d. DO DIFFERENTLY?—Knowing what you know now, what would you do differently in the future? What ideas do you have for improvement? This type of probe uncovers the respondent's *plans for change.*

All these probes keep the channels of communication open and stimulate the respondent to talk.

Nondirective Techniques

1. *Head nod: um huh; encouraging words.* Considerable research has demonstrated that, if the interviewer simply nods his or her head or says "um huh," the respondent will be encouraged to say more. This is a subtle way of showing people that you are paying attention and taking in what they are saying. Specific words of encouragement, such as "that's interesting," or "that sounds like a challenging project," are stronger signs of encouragement and often precede a specific probe.

2. *Paraphrasing ideas.* Here the interviewer briefly restates what the other party has said. This response usually leads to further comments by the interviewee, as illustrated below. It can also be used before a specific probe.

RESPONDENT: "... and I also filled in for the supervisor when she was tied up."

INTERVIEWER: "So you sometimes had supervisory responsibility on this job."

RESPONDENT: "Oh yes, the boss was usually away a couple of days each month and I would handle the work scheduling and also..."

3. *Reflecting feelings.* Every spoken thought has two components: an idea and the speaker's feelings about that idea. Often the feeling component is indifference, but in some interviews very strong feelings can be expressed. It is crucial that the interviewer detect and deal with the respondent's feelings rather than trying to ignore them. This is particularly important in counseling, dis-

ciplinary, and performance appraisal interviews. The emotions of the respondent must be put on the table and dealt with as a part of solving problems and making changes.

> RESPONDENT: "I figured that I couldn't do their work and mine, so I had to stop helping out the other supervisors as much as I used to."

> INTERVIEWER: "You don't sound very happy about that decision."

> RESPONDENT: "I'm not, but I had to cut down. I was spreading myself too thin."

> INTERVIEWER: "Sounds like you felt practically at your wit's end."

> RESPONDENT: "Well, I just couldn't think of anything else to do."

> INTERVIEWER: "You sound pretty frustrated about the whole situation."

> RESPONDENT: "I am. Hell, those guys won't even talk to me anymore."

> INTERVIEWER: "I doubt if that's the reaction you wanted."

> RESPONDENT: "Well no, not at all."

> INTERVIEWER: "Let's see if we can come up with some other ideas of how to handle this predicament. How did you begin reducing the help you gave the other supervisors?"

In this case the respondent is feeling considerable pain and frustration. It is best to acknowledge and deal with these feelings first, and then turn to a rational discussion with a "how" probe.

4. *Summarizing.* This technique has many uses. It is a way for you to check your understanding of what the respondent has said, and it also serves as a stimulus for the respondent to add more.

> INTERVIEWER: "So in essence, you are having difficulty adjusting to this new team member."

> RESPONDENT: "Well, that's part of it, but the addition of
> that person has also altered my job. You see, I used to
> have sole responsibility..."

By summarizing, the interviewer also identified a major theme in the discussion that can be referred to later to focus the conversation.

Summarizing is also useful in making smooth transitions from one topic to another. Notice how the lack of transition in the following example makes the interview rather stilted and awkward.

> RESPONDENT: "... and in addition to my major responsibility
> of supervising the clerks and scheduling their work, I
> also controlled the budget."

> INTERVIEWER: "Um huh, O.K. How much did you get
> involved in the technical detail of your clerks' work?"

The transition in the interview from the supervisory elements of the applicant's job to the technical responsibilities is more smooth with a summary.

> RESPONDENT: "... and in addition to my major responsibility
> of supervising the clerks and scheduling their work, I
> also controlled the budget."

> INTERVIEWER: "So your primary supervisory responsibilities
> were to plan the work day, assign work to each clerk,
> and check their work on a daily basis. You also kept
> the department within budget. Is that correct?"

> RESPONDENT: "Yes."

> INTERVIEWER: "Well, that gives me a good idea of your
> supervisory functions. Let's turn to a related topic. How
> much did you get involved in the actual clerical work
> yourself?"

5. *Pause.* The most purely nondirective technique is the pause, where the interviewer simply says nothing. A ten-second pause puts great pressure on the respondent to say more. While interviewers should use the pause sparingly, you should also avoid feeling

compelled to fill the air with words during occasional lapses in the conversation. Wait it out a few seconds.

These nondirective techniques are important because they stimulate respondents to say more without actually asking them a question. They contribute to the conversational tone of the interview and give it the appearance of being unplanned and unstructured. Too much reliance on direct questions can turn the interview into an interrogation with the emerging sequence of question, answer, question, answer, question, answer. Strive for a mixture of directive and nondirective techniques.

The Interviewer

One critical contributor to the success of the interview that is frequently overlooked is the interviewer's manner. Interviewers need to win the confidence and trust of the person being interviewed, and doing so is unlikely when they speak in a monotone, sit in a slumped position with a bored facial expression, and stare into space. As an interviewer, you need to be more aware of your eye contact, voice, and posture. Try to make personal contact with interviewees by looking them in the eye from time to time and using their names. Since the social acceptability of eye contact varies in different cultures, you need to be aware of what is customary. Furthermore, this should not be carried to excess as in a staring contest, but an appropriate level of eye contact helps to build rapport.

Also try to be aware of your posture and the inflection in your voice. This is especially true for recruiters who interview frequently and who, as representatives of the organization, are trying to attract applicants. A rule of thumb is to let your interest and excitement come through in your voice and posture — lean forward and let your voice rise. Too many interviewers unintentionally lapse into a monotone that may bore the respondent. Listen to yourself and show what you feel. You'll be surprised at how much more positively the other person will respond.

THE PERSONAL TOUCH

As an interviewer, you are a personal link between the applicant or employee being interviewed and the organization you represent. To the other person, that organization and its policies and procedures may appear quite formal and imposing. For example, the job applicant may see the organization mainly as a printed brochure and a confusing series of tests and hurdles between applying for the job and possible employment. As the selection interviewer, you can welcome applicants sincerely and explain the hiring procedures to remove their confusion and apprehension. Similarly, an employee who knows that his or her work is suffering as a result of wrestling with a difficult problem may perceive the company as insensitive and uncaring. As a manager conducting a counseling or performance appraisal interview, however, you can demonstrate that you want to help the employee improve job performance. In short, as an interviewer you have a responsibility to treat interviewees with understanding and respect.

Now I want to be very clear about this point. I'm not proposing that you shirk your other responsibilities as a manager or human resource specialist and be "soft" on interviewees. I want to emphasize, however, that skillful interviewers can meet their objectives and still maintain positive employee relations. Furthermore, if you gain good rapport with interviewees and are perceived as interested and supportive, you will find it easier to meet your objectives.

Selection Interviewing

2

The selection interview is a discussion between an individual applying for a job and a representative of the organization that is hiring. The term "selection interview" is used in the generic sense. Therefore, it may refer to any one of a series of interviews that are used to identify and attract the best applicant for the job. The term refers to the first contact between the two parties, sometimes called the recruiting or screening interview, and it also refers to the final interview before hiring, which usually occurs between applicants and their potential immediate supervisor. Applicants may be from outside the organization, or they may be hoping to change jobs within the organization.

The selection interview is by far the most common of all the interviews discussed in this book. While disciplinary or career planning interviews may be relatively rare in some organizations, there is ample evidence that virtually all organizations use the interview for selection purposes. It may also be argued that the selection interview is the most important of all interviews, because the decision to hire an individual represents a major investment by the employer. Furthermore, the interview is the most widely used and highly trusted of all selection devices. It is the most personal step in the selection process. You may learn *what* an applicant has done on paper, but the interview alone enables you to learn *how, why,* and *how well.* Therefore, in spite of how good applicants may look on paper—résumés, application forms, test scores, letters of recommendation, grade point averages—very nearly all are interviewed by the hiring manager or supervisor and perhaps also by recruiters, human resource specialists, or potential co-workers.

In spite of its widespread use, most managers, supervisors, project leaders, and team members, and human resource specialists have had little or no training in how to plan and conduct selection interviews. Over the past 20 years, participants in my workshops have raised the same types of problems, regardless of how much interviewing experience and training they have had. The most commonly mentioned problems are:

1. Uncertainty about the information they need to gather and how to ask questions to get it

2. Not knowing how to get information without violating Equal Employment Opportunity (EEO) legislation

3. Their own personal attitudes and stereotypes, first-impression biases, and early decisions

4. Quiet, evasive, or polished applicants

5. Lack of skill in breaking through the applicant's facade and prepared answers

6. Not knowing how to evaluate what the applicant says

7. Not knowing how to convert information gathered in the interview into a hiring decision.

I have often been startled by how widespread these problems are and by how little importance managers and their employers seem to place on selection decisions.[1] Groups of technical experts and budget committees spend hours or even days debating over which piece of equipment to purchase for $250,000. Yet, the same organization will invest a comparable amount of money in a new employee ($60,000 in annual salary, plus benefits, for only four years of tenure) after two department members have conducted poorly planned, brief selection interviews with five applicants and have chosen one primarily on the basis of intuition. Choosing the most qualified applicant is a costly, difficult, important business decision, but you can learn how to deal with each of the problems that plague selection interviewers and to ensure that you invest your employer's funds wisely in new employees.

OBJECTIVES

A major reason for the selection interview's popularity is that it meets several objectives of both the interviewer and the applicant. The interviewer has three fundamental goals:

1. *Collect information.* Interviewers need to gather information to answer the following two basic questions:

   a. CAN the applicant DO the job? This involves examining the applicant's experience, training, and education to assess potential to perform specific job responsibilities.

   b. WILL the applicant DO the job? This involves examining the applicant's preferences for and interest in the employment opportunity to determine his or her level of motivation and commitment and estimate how long the applicant will remain in the organization.

2. *Provide information.* Interviewers also inform applicants about the job and organization and try to attract them to accept employment.

3. *Check personal chemistry or organizational culture match.* Interviewers need to learn about the applicant's personal style

and approach to work to judge the fit between the applicant and the organization's culture and determine whether the interviewer and applicant will enjoy working together.

Applicants also have the same three goals:

1. *Present information.* Applicants try to present themselves favorably and sell themselves to the interviewer.

2. *Collect information.* They seek information about the job and organization so they can make an informed decision about accepting employment.

3. *Check personal chemistry.* Applicants also try to assess the culture of the organization and the personal and work styles of the people with whom they may work.

Let's consider the importance of the interviewer's three objectives. Since the interview is a selection device, its primary objective is to collect information from the applicant to predict his or her future job performance and tenure with the organization. Interviewers should devote the majority of their time in the interview to this objective and base their decision to select or reject the applicant on this job-related information. Of secondary importance is the interviewer's objective of presenting information to attract the applicant to accept an offer of employment, and interviewers need to spend some time during the interview to sell the employment opportunity. The *least important* objective is to check personal chemistry. This refers to the highly subjective personal impressions that human beings form when they meet one another, which are strongly influenced by personal factors that may be unrelated to the applicant's potential job performance and tenure with the organization. It is listed as an objective primarily because it is inevitable; all interviewers automatically make subjective judgments about applicants, regardless of how much they try to focus on job-related information. Furthermore, in spite of how good an applicant looks on paper, we all have the human need to look him or her over "person to person" and to determine how that individual will fit in with others in our work group and organization. However, you should assess applicants primarily in job-related terms and minimize the influence of personal chemistry on employment decisions.

A glance at these objectives reveals that the first two on each list may be in conflict, hence making interviewing quite difficult. In objective 1 interviewers are seeking good, predictive information, whereas applicants are trying to sell themselves and look their best. Often the information sent is not that which is needed. This is particularly true as applicants become more skillful at undergoing interviews.

Another point about these objectives is that a two-way selection decision is being made. Not only is the interviewer selecting the applicant, but the applicant is also selecting the organization. Therefore, in objective 2, applicants may have to sift through the interviewer's presentation of the position and company to decide if this is the kind of employment opportunity they really want. When qualified applicants are scarce, interviewers may increase their emphasis on objective 2 to attract applicants to their organization. They must be careful, however, in how strongly they emphasize the positive aspects of the job and organization and how much negative information they withhold. Research has shown that presenting *realistic* information about the job and company reduces the percentage of applicants who accept an offer of employment, but is also related to longer tenure among those who actually accept the offer.[2] Furthermore, at least one newly hired employee has won a court case and $67,000 in damages against a Canadian employer that promised a more positive employment opportunity in a selection interview than it actually delivered.[3] Interviewers should present employment opportunities as positively as possible, but without misrepresenting the facts.

The objectives also place interviewers in a rather divided position. In objective 1 interviewers carefully examine applicants to learn whether they can and will do the job, but in objective 2 they also try to attract applicants. Interviewers must sometimes ask difficult questions to assess the applicant's true potential and intentions, but they must do so in a relatively unstressful manner because they want all applicants to leave the interview with a favorable impression of their organization. This dual purpose of scrutinizing and attracting the applicant requires a high level of skill from interviewers.

Furthermore, many supervisors and managers place too much emphasis on selling the job to the applicant and too little emphasis on examining the applicant's potential and willingness to perform the job. In short, they *talk* too much, *learn* too little, and are forced to make their decision on the basis of personal chemistry. All interviewers should place sufficient emphasis on objective 1, gathering information from the applicant, to ensure effective selection decisions.

All these objectives must be met if any selection interview is to be effective, although some may be emphasized more than others, depending on the nature of the employer, job, and labor market. The selection interview definitely fulfills some of these objectives better than others. It allows both parties to test personal chemistry and provides an excellent format in which the interviewer and applicant can exchange useful information about the nature of the employment opportunity. As a predictive device that contributes to the selection decision, however, the interview has had only limited success. In short, the interviewer's assessment of the applicant is very poorly related to that applicant's actual job performance after being hired.

CORRECTING THE SELECTION INTERVIEW'S WEAKNESSES

I believe in the selection interview. It can be an effective tool for meeting its primary objective—choosing the best applicant for the job. But, as commonly practiced, the selection interview often does not meet this objective. The failure of the interview to predict future job performance can typically be traced to how the interview was designed and conducted. This chapter focuses on the two essential ingredients of an effective interview: *content* and *conducting*. As noted in Chapter 1, content refers to the topics covered in the interview and the questions that are asked. Conducting refers to how the interviewer covers content, for example, guiding the conversation, getting applicants to volunteer needed information, and probing for more detail to ensure a valid selection decision.

Let's begin with the content of the selection interview—how it is planned and designed. This is its Achilles heel. Most people, be they managers, supervisors, project leaders, team members, or human resource specialists, communicate relatively well, but they know too little about which topics to cover in the selection interview and, in the context of EEO, which topics to avoid. Table 2.1 covers four major weaknesses of the interview, and ways in which these weaknesses can be minimized are summarized in Table 2.2.

The interview is probably the most thoroughly researched and yet most poorly applied of all available selection devices. Beginning as early as 1915,[4] literally thousands of studies have examined the frailties of the selection interview. The conclusions of this vast body of research have been resoundingly negative. Major reviews[5] have stated and restated that the selection interview has low reliability and low predictive validity. Low reliability means that different interviewers do not agree in their assessments of the same applicant. Low predictive validity means that there is only a weak statistical relationship between an interviewer's assessment of an applicant's potential to succeed in a job and that applicant's actual performance after being hired. In short, the interview fails to predict future job performance.

Of course, since human behavior is impossible to predict with complete accuracy, no selection device can predict future job performance for all applicants. But the interview's validity can be improved when interviewers carefully prepare its content and pursue job-related information during the interview. This is encouraging, because it means that an awareness of the pitfalls

Table 2.1
WEAKNESSES OF THE SELECTION INTERVIEW

I. **Planning Is Poor**

    A. Interviewers do not know their objectives

    B. Interviewers do not plan and structure the interview

    C. Interviewers do not know the job for which the candidate is applying

II. **Approach Is Psychiatric**

    A. Interviewers assume the role of amateur psychiatrist

    B. Applicant is evaluated on inappropriate criteria

III. **Interviewers Are Human Beings**

    A. Personal attitudes and stereotypes abound

    B. Interviewers overemphasize negative information

    C. Interviewers forget

IV. **Interviewers Violate EEO Guidelines**

    A. Interviewers raise prohibited topics

    B. Evaluations are based on information that is not clearly job-related

---

of the selection interview can help you to develop more effective interviews. Let's take a look at some of the major pitfalls.

Poor Versus Proper Planning

Many selection interviews are simply not carefully planned. With their busy schedules, recruiters or human resource specialists find themselves facing an applicant before they have had much time to think carefully about the interview they are about to conduct. Because they see job applicants infrequently, managers,

26

Table 2.2

**IMPROVING THE INTERVIEW
AS A SELECTION DEVICE**

I. **Plan Properly**

   A. Know your objectives
   B. Plan an interview format to meet those objectives
   C. Know as much as possible about the job to be filled

II. **Make the Evaluation Process More Job-related**

   A. Evaluate the applicant in terms of potential to perform job-related functions
   B. Evaluate the applicant's willingness to work for your organization
   C. Record additional comments

III. **Build a Better Interview**

   A. Whenever possible, tailor the interview to a specific job
   B. Systematically cover all relevant topics in the interview
   C. Record your evaluations and supportive documentation

IV **Ensure that Interviewers Conform to EEOC Guidelines**

   A. When in doubt, don't ask
   B. Ask questions in job-related terms
   C. Document your selection decisions

---

supervisors, project leaders, and team members may also take little time to plan a selection interview.

The interview is likely to fail if interviewers do not know their objectives and do not develop a plan to meet those objectives. Lack of planning usually leads to a relatively unstructured interview, in which whatever comes up automatically becomes the content of today's interview. Lack of structure creates major problems because the less structured the interview is, the less reliable and valid it will be.[6] Furthermore, an unstructured interview enables interviewers to confirm their own biases, stereotypes, and first impressions and is subject to charges of discrimination. Finally, since the major objective of the selection interview is to choose the person most qualified to do the job, the *interviewer's* knowledge of the job is crucial. The less you know about the job to be filled, the less qualified you are to examine the applicant's potential to perform that job successfully and to make a valid selection decision. Therefore, recruiters should be drawn from the applicant's technical discipline, and managers and supervisors should conduct final selection interviews and make the hiring decision. With their excellent working knowledge of the job to be filled, they are in the best position to assess the applicant's potential to perform job responsibilities.

Developing a general plan for the selection interview is relatively straightforward. Interviewers must know their objectives and then design the interview so that each objective is met. They must know as much as possible about the job in question. The best approach is a *semistructured* one in which the main parts of the interview are laid out in order, but which still allows interviewers to pursue topics in a flexible manner. Here is a suggestion for the overall format of the selection interview.

1. *Establish rapport.* Begin by introducing yourself and stating the job and organization you are representing. Next, welcome the applicant warmly; making small talk will help to set him or her at ease. (The small talk is optional; avoid picking a topic at random because it will appear forced.) Study the résumé or application form beforehand and look for something in common: a hobby, interest, person, school, or part of the country. This gives you a good place to begin your small talk.

2. *Set the agenda.* It is helpful to outline your plan for the interview for two reasons. First, it can help to relax applicants by letting them know what's coming. Second, it puts you firmly in control by providing a road map to be followed, and therefore

discourages game-playing applicants from trying to take control of the interview themselves. You can set the agenda simply by summarizing the next three steps; for example, "In the next 40 minutes I will begin by asking you a number of questions. Then I'll tell you more about the job and our organization. Later on in the interview I'll give you an opportunity to ask me any questions that I have not already answered. I'll be jotting down a few notes during our conversation."

3. *Gather information.* Here is where the primary objectives of both the interviewer and applicant are met. This is the detailed discussion of the applicant's past that helps the interviewer determine whether the applicant is suitable for the job. It is in this section that you will answer the two questions, *"Can* the applicant do the job?" and *"Will* the applicant do the job?" (This part of the interview is covered in more detail later in this chapter.)

4. *Describe the organization, department, job, and conditions of employment.* This is the section of the interview in which you inform and attract the applicant. Present a realistic, positive picture of the nature of the organization, the department, and the specific job to ensure that the applicant makes an informed decision. In addition, explain the conditions under which employees work (e.g., overtime, travel, stress, changing priorities). This will help applicants decide whether they are interested in joining your organization. Although some interviewers present this information before gathering information from the applicant, it is better not to do this. By describing the job *before* stage 3, you may be playing into the hands of game-playing applicants by inadvertently coaching them on what aspects of their background to stress to present themselves as favorably as possible.

5. *Answer questions.* This stage is directed toward the applicant's objective to learn about the employment opportunity. Although your presentation may be thorough, you should give applicants a chance to raise additional questions.

6. *Terminate.* Simply thanking applicants for their time and telling them what will happen next (e.g., "We'll be interviewing

for the next two weeks and will telephone you with our decision within the next three weeks") is an honest and comfortable way to end the interview.

As mentioned earlier, many supervisors and managers spend too much time talking in the selection interview (Stage 4) and do not learn enough from the applicant in Stage 3. Selection interviewers should spend 75% of their time collecting information from the applicant. The presentation of information to the applicant should take no more than five to ten minutes in the selection interview.

PSYCHIATRIC VERSUS JOB-RELATED EVALUATIONS IN THE INTERVIEW

Probably the greatest weakness in selection interviewing is the way in which we human beings evaluate one another. All too often interviewers try to assess an applicant's basic character in half an hour. Highly subjective judgments are made about the applicant's personality traits as well as his or her skills and knowledge. Although there is no way to eliminate subjectivity from the selection interview, these evaluations of the applicant are often far more subjective than they need be. Let's examine more closely the evaluation process in Figure 2.1.

All interviewers have at their disposal the same three basic sources of information that relate to whether the applicant can do and will do the job. This information can be directly heard or observed by the interviewer. These three sources are:

1. *Previous work and non-work experience*—activities the applicant has performed in paid or unpaid settings (e.g., extracurricular activities and hobbies) that may be related to the responsibilities of the job to be filled.

2. *Previous training and education*—job-related activities the applicant has learned to do.

Figure 2.1
THE EVALUATION PROCESS

BEHAVIOR

What Applicant Has Done or Is Doing
1. Previous work and non-work experience
2. Previous education and training
3. Demonstrated behavior and stated preferences and intentions during the interview

Psychiatric Approach

Job-Related Approach

PERSONALITY TRAITS

What Applicant Is

1. Maturity
2. Intelligence
3. Attitude
4. Aggressiveness
5. Personality
6. Confidence
7. Judgment
8. Appearance

BEHAVIOR

What Applicant CAN DO and WILL DO After Being Hired

CAN DO—SAMPLE JOB: SENIOR SYSTEMS ANALYST/MIS DEPARTMENT

1. Resolve application problems on a 24-hour basis during critical production cycles.
2. Develop written system/PGM specifications for other team members.
3. Develop and administer work plans for other team members, utilizing project management tools under imposed regulatory deadlines.
4. Analyze requested modifications to existing systems.
5. Analyze, design, and implement computer systems.
6. Communicate project status to end users and MIS management verbally and in writing.
7. Provide technical guidance to team members.
8. Direct the work of junior team members.
9. Share in programming responsibilities when necessary.
10. Set priorities and schedule work and time under constantly changing conditions.

WILL DO

1. Degree of Interest in the Company, Department, and Job
2. Clarity of Career Goals
3. Level of Motivation

31

3. *Demonstrated behavior and stated preferences and intentions during the interview*—Interviewers can directly observe the applicant perform some job-related activities such as dealing with stress and presenting ideas orally. In addition, applicants can express their preferences for specific job functions and working conditions, as well as their career plans.

Amateur psychiatry. These sources of information are shown at the top of Figure 2.1. Interviewers have two choices of how they use this information to evaluate the applicant. One common choice is on the left side of the figure, the *psychiatric approach to evaluation.* With this approach, interviewers infer from what applicants have done and said what kind of people they are, in terms of ratings of basic traits and characteristics. This amateur psychiatry is encouraged by applicant evaluation forms on which interviewers rate applicants in terms of their level of initiative, aggressiveness, maturity, stability, emotional adjustment, intelligence, and the like.

There are major problems with this type of evaluation process. These traits are quite vague and poorly defined; what may be positively regarded as initiative by one interviewer may be negatively interpreted as aggressiveness by another. Furthermore, traits are not observed directly. We do not see initiative or maturity or intelligence. What we actually see is behavior from which we infer or conclude the presence of an underlying trait. There is a great deal of subjectivity in this evaluation process, and consequently bias can strongly influence the ratings. Much of the unreliability of selection interviews stems from this type of evaluation. Simply put, this evaluation process puts interviewers in the realm of the unseen and undefined—they act as amateur psychiatrists, judging the basic character of applicants.

Most interviewers are not trained to make these kinds of assessments, nor are they comfortable trying to do so. Unfortunately, many training courses and books on selection interviewing propose long lists of questions to probe ambiguous personal traits of questionable job relevance (e.g., "do you prefer to work alone or in a group, do you make friends easily, what kind of people do you enjoy being around most, how would a friend describe you, and if you could control what people said behind your back what would you like them to be saying about you?").[7] These questions, and additional examples in Table 2.3, merely invite applicants to game-play and provide little indication of their potential for successful job performance.

Job-related evaluation. Now let's move to the right side of Figure 2.1. The primary objective of the selection interview is to collect information to determine whether the applicant can do and will do the job. Ultimately, any selection decision is at least implicitly a prediction of future job performance.[8] When interviewers send applicants on to testing, another interview, or the job, they do so because they think the applicant can and will perform at an acceptable level on a specific job.

This leads us to a more *job-related* way of evaluating applicants. Interviewers can use behavior—past and present—to predict future performance. The predicted job performance can be broken down into major job responsibilities such as those in Figure 2.1. To assess whether applicants *can do* the job, interviewers need to probe into the three sources of information listed earlier (previous work and non-work experience, training and education, and actual behavior in the interview), and evaluate applicants' potential to perform specific job responsibilities. To assess whether applicants *will do* the job, interviewers need to probe into applicants' preferences and intentions and whether they have worked under specific working conditions (overtime, travel, stress, changing priorities) in the past. Interviewers can record these evaluations of CAN DO and WILL DO on an Applicant Evaluation Form shown in Figure 2.2.

A point of clarification is needed here. I am not saying that what a person is, in terms of personal traits, does not influence job performance. I am saying that a concerted effort to assess an applicant's personal traits with a number of psychological questions is *not necessary* to make a selection decision. The left side of Figure 2.1, with its detailed rating of personal traits, is unnecessary.

Table 2.3
INAPPROPRIATE QUESTIONS OFTEN ASKED
BY SELECTION INTERVIEWERS

I. **Too General; these questions turn control
    of the interview over to the applicant.**

    1. Tell me about yourself.
    2. Why should I hire you?
    3. What qualifications do you have that make you think you
        will be successful in business?
    4. What do you think it takes to be successful in a company
        like ours?
    5. In what ways do you think you can make a contribution
        to our company?
    6. What qualities should a successful manager possess?
    7. If you were hiring someone for this position, what qualities
        would you look for?

II. **Too Obvious; these questions invite
    canned answers.**

    1. What do you expect to be earning in five years?
    2. Which is more important to you, money or the type of
        work?
    3. What do you consider to be your greatest strengths and
        weaknesses?
    4. How would you describe yourself?
    5. How do you think someone who knows you well would
        describe you?
    6. What motivates you to put forth your greatest effort?
    7. How do your determine or evaluate success?
    8. Describe the relationship that should exist between a supervisor
        and those reporting to him or her.
    9. How would you describe the ideal job for you?

(cont.)

Table 2.3 (cont.)

III. Too Psychological; these questions measure little that is related to job performance.

1. What two or three accomplishments have given you the most satisfaction? Why?
2. Describe your most rewarding college or work experience.
3. What do you really want to do in life?
4. What changes would you make in your university or employer? Why?
5. What do you see yourself doing five years from now?

In practice, these assessments happen automatically as two strangers meet and form impressions of one another. These assessments meet the third objective of the selection interview—namely, testing personal chemistry—and can be recorded as "Additional Comments" on the Applicant Evaluation Form in Figure 2.2. But an interview that merely tests personal chemistry is very likely to fail as a selection device because it will not meet the objective of gathering information to determine whether the applicant can and will perform the job successfully. Designing and conducting selection interviews that predict future job performance from past and current behavior will ensure high levels of reliability and predictive validity. (This is described in detail later in the chapter.) First, however, we need to consider another major problem in selection interviewing.

Interviewer's Bias

Most people like to think of themselves as good judges of character, and many are. But people judge character in different ways and with different standards, and this spells unreliability. There is no escaping the conclusion that a major problem with the selection interview is the interviewer. The interviewer is a

Figure 2.2
APPLICANT EVALUATION FORM

Applicant's Name

Interviewer

APPLICANT'S QUALIFICATIONS

Education _____ Years of Relevant Work Experience _____

A.	EVALUATION OF APPLICANT'S POTENTIAL TO PERFORM	Please Circle Your Evaluation

Please Circle Your Evaluation
High   Low

Major Responsiblities

	High				Low
1. _____	5	4	3	2	1
2. _____	5	4	3	2	1
3. _____	5	4	3	2	1
4. _____	5	4	3	2	1
5. _____	5	4	3	2	1
6. _____	5	4	3	2	1
7. _____	5	4	3	2	1
8. _____	5	4	3	2	1
9. _____	5	4	3	2	1

B. APPLICANT'S WORK INTEREST AND CAREER DIRECTION

Please Circle Your Evaluation
High   Low

	High				Low
1. Interest in the Organization	5	4	3	2	1
2. Interest in the Position	5	4	3	2	1
3. Motivation	5	4	3	2	1
4. Clarity of Career Goals	5	4	3	2	1

C. ADDITIONAL COMMENTS

_____

_____

_____

D. INTERVIEW RESULT

Please Circle Your Evaluation

	Definitely Hire		Marginal		Reject
1. Recommendation for Hire	5	4	3	2	1

human being and is therefore susceptible to a number of influences that bias judgments about an applicant and therefore undermine the reliability and predictive validity of the interview.

Interviewers' attitudes and backgrounds contribute to low reliability by affecting their interpretation of what applicants say and their subsequent evaluation of the applicants.[9] It is known that interviewers have a relatively well-defined stereotype of the ideal applicant. Furthermore, those stereotypes of ideal applicants for the same job may differ among interviewers, and the applicant information interviewers focus on differs according to the person who conducts the interviews.[10]

These biases are complicated further by the tendency to place more emphasis on negative rather than positive information since the decision to hire an applicant who fails on the job is riskier to the interviewer and the employer than the decision to reject an applicant who would have succeeded.[11] Furthermore, if the interviewer uncovers negative information *early* in the interview and forms a negative first impression of the applicant, the final decision is more likely to be negative. Since negative first impressions are often based on an applicant's appearance (e.g., dress, firmness of handshake, hair style, sex, age, race), which is not related to job performance, many interviewers make premature decisions to reject applicants unfairly. These decisions based on negative first impressions are most likely to occur in an unstructured interview.

Forgetting is another important source of error in interviews.[12] Interviewers simply forget much of what they hear. Furthermore, if two interviewers remember *different* information about an applicant, their evaluations of that applicant can differ. A major problem in selection interviewing is the tendency of human beings to distort, ignore, forget, or otherwise waste important information.

Building a Better Interview

To remedy this problem, either the interviewer or the interview must change. As long as people conduct interviews, the problems of stereotypes, emphasizing the negative, first impressions, forgetting, and other forms of bias will persist. Therefore, a more fruitful alternative is to create an interview that minimizes the effects of these human frailties. In short, you must build a better interview.

To do this, you need to design an interview for a specific job or job family and assess applicants in terms of the potential they show to perform that job. This puts emphasis on the right side of Figure 2.1. You already know that reliability and predictive validity increase when the interview is structured and when the interviewer has knowledge about the job to be filled. Therefore, you are more likely to succeed if you prepare and conduct interviews that are *tailored to the job* in question. The focus of the typical psychiatric interview is on questions like, "What kind of person is this? What are his or her basic personality traits?" In the tailored interview the focus is on different questions, such as, "On the basis of what these applicants are saying and doing, how well can they perform these major job responsibilities? How will her previous work experience help her do these aspects of the job? Has he had any training and education that he can apply to this job?" This approach leads to a different interview with a somewhat different focus for each job to be filled.

DESIGNING THE TAILORED INTERVIEW

How can you go about designing and conducting tailored interviews? Try the following steps. It should be emphasized that these guidelines are intended to produce only a part of the entire selection interview, the part that collects information to determine whether the applicant can do the job. This is phase 3 of the overall interview format described earlier.

Step 1: Start with the job. Too often when managers, supervisors, project leaders, team members, or human resource specialists are planning an interview, they think in terms of the kind of person they want or the qualities and skills of the successful applicant. This is not wrong; it's simply premature. The first thought should be about the job to be filled. To select someone, you must first know your objective—job performance. You do not hire employees for their personality traits, knowledge, or skills, and so forth, but ultimately *to perform*. Therefore, you should start by conducting a job analysis and listing the major responsibilities that make up the job. Most jobs can be broken down into five to ten major responsibilities. For example, the sample job in the right side of Figure 2.1 was divided into ten major responsibilities. Let's have a closer look at them.

Sample Job: Senior Systems Analyst— MIS Department

1. Resolve application problems on a 24-hour basis during critical production cycles.
2. Develop written system/PGM specifications for other team members.
3. Develop and administer work plans for other team members, utilizing project management tools under imposed regulatory deadlines.
4. Analyze requested modifications to existing systems.
5. Analyze, design, and implement computer systems.
6. Communicate project status to end users and MIS management verbally and in writing.
7. Provide technical guidance to team members.
8. Direct the work of junior team members.
9. Share in programming responsibilities when necessary.
10. Set priorities and schedule work and time under constantly changing conditions.

Notice that each major responsibility begins with an action verb, followed by what is acted upon, which is then followed by additional information about the context of the job in question. Hence, we specify in the sixth major responsibility that this job requires the potential to communicate project status to certain people—both end users and MIS management—in certain ways—verbally and in writing. In the interview you need to assess an applicant's previous experience in this activity or knowledge of how to go about it. Each major responsibility is a standard against which each applicant is evaluated. The more precise and clearly defined the standard is, the easier task you will have in evaluating the applicant's potential to meet that standard successfully.

The major responsibilities are in behavioral terms. Each refers to what employees do, not who they are. If your organization has position descriptions, they will be helpful in identifying the major responsibilities to be assessed in the selection interview for a specific job opening. You can enter the major responsibilities for a given job in Section A of the Applicant Evaluation Form in Figure 2.2, and each interviewer can independently evaluate the applicant in terms of his or her potential to perform those responsibilities.

Step 2: Write hypothetical situations. A semistructured approach is best. Do not enter the interview with a lengthy list of prepared questions. Later in this chapter, I will discuss how you can phrase questions to assess the applicant's potential to perform the responsibilities of the job to be filled. However, you should enter the interview with a small number of specially prepared questions, called *hypothetical situations*—one for each of the two or three most important job responsibilities. These hypothetical questions are brief descriptions of a situation or problem that a new employee might encounter which would challenge him or her to perform the job responsibility well. The following is an example for "Set priorities and schedule work and time under constantly changing conditions":

> You have made plans for a six-month project based upon preliminary requirements established by management, but when the final requirements are issued, you learn that they have changed significantly and the completion date is one month sooner than you expected. What would you do?

These hypothetical situations essentially *simulate* a part of the job and ask applicants to tell you how they would handle problems or challenges. They would not necessarily be used with every applicant. (There is an explanation of how and when you can use them in the part of this chapter dealing with conducting the selection interview.)

SELECTION INTERVIEWING AND THE LAW

So far, this chapter has shown how you can avoid several pitfalls that undermine the effectiveness of the selection interview by knowing your objectives, using job-related criteria to evaluate applicants, and tailoring the interview to the job. There is one final pitfall of which all selection interviewers must be aware to ensure that the content of their interviews is beyond reproach.

Since 1915 evidence has accumulated that the interview, as commonly practiced, is not a very effective selection device. The continued use of invalid interviews has cost organizations significantly. Applicants who were capable of performing successfully on the job have been rejected, and others have been hired only to fail to perform well. Since the middle 1960s, however, poorly trained interviewers may have led to costs far greater than poor use of human resources. A large body of legislation, executive orders, and regulations of the federal, state, and city governments now makes every selection interviewer liable for a suit against his or her organization for discrimination against applicants on the basis of race, color, religion, sex, national origin, mental or physical handicap, disability (including AIDS), marital status, pregnancy, veteran status, or age. Let's begin by summarizing the major legislation; then we will discuss how it influences the selection interviewing process.[13]

The most publicized federal law and the one most often cited by persons who feel they have been discriminated against is Title VII of the *Civil Rights Act of 1964*, as amended by the

Equal Employment Opportunity Act of 1972. This federal legislation prohibits discrimination in employment with respect to the terms, conditions, and privileges of employment on the basis of race, color, religion, sex, or national origin. This is the broadest of the equal employment opportunity (EEO) laws and covers such areas of employment as selection, job assignments, training programs, promotion, and discipline.

The Age Discrimination in Employment Act of 1967, as amended in 1978, is a federal law that prohibits discrimination against applicants and employees over 39 years old in terms of hiring, compensation, discharge, and other major aspects of employment. The statute requires a company to judge an applicant without any consideration of age. Although work experience is a legitimate factor to consider in any employment decision, the fact that an employee "has been around for a long time" and is over the age of 39 is prohibited to be taken into account in a manner that adversely affects the employee.

The Vocational Rehabilitation Act of 1973 makes it illegal for companies with federal contracts and subcontracts to discriminate against a physically or mentally handicapped person for reasons that have nothing to do with his or her ability to perform the job. Furthermore, Section 503 of the act requires such companies to take affirmative action to employ and advance in employment qualified handicapped individuals. This same section dictates that federal contractors make reasonable accommodation for the physical and mental limitations of an employee or an applicant for employment. *The Pregnancy Discrimination Act of 1978* also prohibits private employers of 15 or more employees from discriminating because of pregnancy, childbirth, and related conditions.

The Vietnam-Era Veterans Readjustment Assistance Act of 1974 forbids employment discrimination against veterans of the Vietnam era and all disabled veterans. Moreover, this act requires that all organizations with government contracts take affirmative action to employ and advance in employment such individuals.

The Americans with Disabilities Act of 1990 has been called the most sweeping civil rights legislation since the Civil Rights Act of 1964. This law prohibits all employers, including privately owned businesses and local governments, from discriminating against disabled employees or job applicants when making employment decisions. It also requires that employers make "reasonable accommodation" to disabled employees and job applicants so long as this doesn't inflict "undue hardship" on the business. This legislation defines disability as a physical or mental impairment that substantially limits an individual's major life activities. It also protects individuals who have AIDS or the AIDS virus against discrimination.

The Civil Rights Act of 1991 strengthens previous civil rights legislation by adding remedies for discrimination based on sex, disability, religion, or national origin that had previously applied only to employment discrimination based on race. This new law adds jury trials to determine liability and compensatory and punitive damages in cases involving *intentional* violations of Title VII of the Civil Rights Act of 1964 and the Americans with Disabilities Act of 1990. The law also requires employers to demonstrate that employment practices are job-related to the position in question and consistent with business necessity, *even though they are not intended to be discriminatory.*

IMPLICATIONS OF EEO LEGISLATION

This legislation and succeeding court decisions apply to all steps in the selection process, including employment advertising and information collected by way of application forms, employment tests, reference checks, and the interview. Since so many applicants now fall into a protected group, employers need to be cautious in their hiring practices to avoid charges of discrimination.

Simply stated, Title VII and most of the other laws prohibit two main types of employment policies and practices. The first type are policies or practices that treat some individuals worse than others because of prohibited personal characteristics. This is called *disparate treatment*. Disparate treatment occurs, for example, when a white, male manager conducts thorough 45-minute interviews with white, male applicants and cursory, much shorter interviews with black or female applicants.

The second type of prohibited employer conduct is that which generates an unjustifiable, disproportionately negative effect on any individual or group of applicants for employment who are members of a protected class. This type of behaviour is said to produce a *disparate impact* that is not justified by the employer's legitimate need to operate a safe, efficient, or profitable business. In other words, if employment records show that an employer has hired a greater percentage of white applicants than, for example, black or female applicants, then the hiring practice is said to have a disparate impact on the protected group. A difference in percentages, however, does not necessarily prove that the employer has discriminated illegally against the protected group. If a greater percentage of white applicants is also more highly qualified than the black or female applicants, the hiring practices are job-related and may therefore be justified.

In determining whether illegal discrimination has occurred, the courts have typically considered the effects on results of the practice or policy, *not the intent*. Most interviewers do not intentionally discriminate against women and minorities. Acting in good faith, however, does not necessarily constitute an acceptable defense to a charge of discrimination. Thus, questioning techniques (e.g., asking for an applicant's age or religion) and subtle inferences that interviewers apply to some groups of applicants (e.g., a female applicant is more likely to quit or require time off to raise children than would a male applicant) may be discriminating *in their effect*.

The "burden of proof" is a critical consideration in discrimination cases. Title VII is a complaint-oriented law. That is to say, any person who feels he or she has been discriminated against may file a complaint with the government against the employer. When a complaint is filed, the Equal Employment Opportunity

Commission (EEOC), created by Title VII to enforce the law, sends a notice to the employer and initiates an investigation of the complaint to discover if there does exist a sufficient basis in fact to support the allegations contained in the complaint. Title VII grants to the EEOC broad investigatory power and access to all relevant employment records and documents and can therefore generate major administrative costs for an organization under investigation. A comparable agency, the Office of Federal Contract Compliance Programs (OFCCP), has jurisdiction over employers with federal contracts.

If the EEOC or OFCCP finds there is reasonable cause to believe that illegal discrimination has taken place (analysis of hiring records shows statistical disparate impact), it will so notify the employer and attempt to settle the complaint through conciliation. If this attempt at settlement fails, then the EEOC, the OFCCP, or the charging party may file a lawsuit against the employer. Such legal action could result in forced "quota" hiring, reinstatement, loss of a federal contractor's privileges of doing business with the government, or punitive damages for the suing party as well as for numerous other individuals if it is a lawsuit involving a whole group of applicants.

A crucial aspect of this legislation is how the courts determine which party should bear the responsibility to prove that illegal discrimination has or has not occurred when an individual files suit against an employer. Until 1989, the courts favored the complainant. Once disparate impact had been documented, the courts required the employer to demonstrate that its employment practices were related to applicants' potential job performance, rather than to personal characteristics of the applicants. *In other words, the employer had to prove its innocence.* But a series of Supreme Court decisions, most from 1989, placed the burden of proof on the complainant. In the 1989 case of *Wards Cove Packing Co. v. Atonio,* the Supreme Court ruled that the complainant had to prove that the employer had intentionally favored whites in its hiring practices. This reversal of precedent by the Supreme Court provided a major impetus for the Civil Rights Act of 1991, which has again placed the burden of proof on the employer. This law requires an employer to defend itself against a charge of unintentional discrimination by demonstrating that the practice leading to disparate impact against a protected group is clearly job-related and consistent with business necessity. Therefore, federal law now requires employers to prove that they are innocent of charges of employment discrimination, and the Civil Rights Act of 1991 is expected to increase the number of lawsuits for alleged discrimination.

Effects of EEO Legislation on Selection Interviewing

Whether the burden of proof in discrimation cases is on the employer or the complainant, these federal laws and Supreme Court decisions have significant implications for all employers and their selection interviewers. In particular they affect the kind of information interviewers collect in the selection interview, the questions they ask, the basis for their employment decisions, and the records they keep to support their decisions.

Information Collected in the Interview

Extensive legislation prohibits withholding employment from applicants on the basis of race, color, religion, sex, national origin, mental or physical handicap, disability (including AIDS) marital status, pregnancy, veteran status, or age. Quite simply, these acts restrict the topics selection interviewers may discuss; that is, the questions they may legally ask. Questions that appear to be entirely innocent and naive may cost an employer a lawsuit. A conservative rule of thumb is, *When in doubt, don't ask.* Many managers, supervisors, and human resource specialists become annoyed with what they perceive as extreme restrictions imposed by EEO legislation. But remember, this legislation has typically favored the complainant. If a topic is raised in the interview, it may influence the decision to hire or reject an applicant. The only way in which you can prove that your employment decisions did not discriminate against protected classes of applicants is *not* to have discussed the topics that would identify the applicant as a member of that protected class.

A more positive way of viewing EEO guidelines is to ask yourself what possible relevance could these topics have to job performance. If your objective is to identify people who can and will do the job, EEO legislation does not restrict you from any *job-related* source of information. The key is knowing what not to ask, and also knowing how to gather the information you really need. Let's have a look at some potentially troublesome topics.

1. Birthplace
2. Birthplace of parents, spouse, or other close relatives
3. If applicant is a naturalized citizen
4. Foreign languages applicant reads, writes, and speaks fluently
5. How applicant acquired fluency in foreign languages
6. Wife's maiden name
7. Mother's maiden name

All these topics are questionable and should be avoided except in special circumstances because they all provide information about an applicant's national origin and ethnic background. If the job requires fluency in a foreign language, question 4 is acceptable, but question 5 might reveal that the applicant was born outside the United States. You might be interested in learning about all of this information as you get to know a person, *but not in the selection interview.* That's the key.

You may legally inquire into an applicant's right to work in the United States. This can be legally established through such inquiries as

8. Asking if the applicant is a U.S. citizen
9. Asking to see the applicant's permanent residence visa

Consider the following:

10. If applicant has ever worked under another name
11. Marital status
12. Plans for marriage or pregnancy
13. Number of children
14. If applicant has child care problems
15. Information regarding spouse's job plans

Each of the inquiries may be interpreted as discriminating against women or married people. These topics may all be relevant, however, to the applicant's *willingness* to do the job. That is, they may interfere with an applicant's willingness to meet specific conditions of employment, such as working overtime, traveling, working shifts, relocating, and working weekends. This brings us to a fundamental point about legal restrictions on the selection interview. *You are permitted to ask for any truly relevant information you need, so long as you ask the questions in job-related terms, not personal terms.* For example,

> Don't ask a female applicant if she is married,
> Do ask all applicants if they are able to relocate, work an average of one weekend per month, or take three-day business trips twice a month.

> Don't ask if a female applicant has child care problems,
> Do ask all applicants if they can work late on one-hour's notice at least four times a month.

Now let's take a look at another set of topics:

16. If applicant has ever been arrested
17. Type of discharge from the military service
18. Names of clubs, societies, or lodges to which applicant belongs
19. Whether applicant owns a car
20. Whether applicant lives in a house or an apartment
21. Whether applicant owns or rents a home

Each of these topics may contribute to disparate impact on a protected class of employees. That is, screening applicants on these topics may lead to an unjustifiable negative effect on a protected group. For example, blacks and Hispanics, compared with whites, are more likely to have been arrested (without necessarily having been convicted) or to have received a dishonorable discharge from military service. Employers who screen out applicants on these grounds had better be prepared to demonstrate that doing so leads to high levels of job performance. Similarly, questions 18–21 reflect socioeconomic status and may therefore be seen as having disparate impact against blacks and certain ethnic groups. These topics should be avoided in the interview.

Medical questions, even though job-related, should not be addressed during the interview, and medical examinations cannot be required during the selection process because they may reveal other prohibited information, such as age, color, and sex. Therefore, interviewers should not ask questions about

22. Height and weight

23. If applicant has a disability

24. If applicant has AIDS or other serious diseases

Virtually all U.S. employers make the offer of employment *contingent* on the applicant passing a medical examination. That is, after the applicant has passed all other selection hurdles and has been offered the job, a physician can examine the person for any mental or physical factors that would *genuinely interfere* with effective job performance. Simply having a disability is not grounds for disqualifying an applicant.

Finally, interviewers may not legally ask the applicant's age. Interviewers may ask, however, for verification that the applicant is over a minimum age for the job to be filled.

What Can Be Asked?

The subject of EEO guidelines and restrictions is often rather exasperating to interviewers because the emphasis is quite negative.

After hearing all the topics they cannot discuss, some interviewers feel like throwing up their hands and asking, "What's left for me to talk about?" The answer is brief but truly offers a great deal of fruitful territory. Interviewers should focus on:

1. What the applicant has done in the past—this includes previous work experience and also non-work experience such as extracurricular activities, hobbies, and interests in which the applicant may have performed functions that could be used on the job.

2. What the applicant has learned in the past—this includes formal education and course work as well as training courses in which the applicant may have learned something that could be applied to the job.

3. Applicant's preferences, interests, and intentions—this includes the work and non-work activities the applicant liked or disliked in the past, courses of particular interest to the applicant, and his or her long-term career plans. Also included are the working conditions to which the applicant has been exposed in the past.

A semistructured interview that has been tailored to the job will enable you to probe the first two points to assess whether the applicant can do the job and the third to assess whether he or she will do the job. If you follow the approach recommended in this chapter, you will have a great deal to talk about, and you should have no EEO problems.

Basis for the Evaluation

The most significant influence of EEO legislation on the selection process concerns the basis on which the selection decision is made. The acts cited earlier state explicitly that people cannot be denied employment on the basis of a long list of personal characteristics.

In the selection interview, this legislation relates directly to the basis on which the applicant is evaluated. The interview is the most highly subjective of all available selection devices and is therefore most open to claims of discrimination. Even careful avoidance of the topics itemized in the last section may not be an adequate defense. This is because age, sex, physical or mental handicap, color, disability, race, and ethnic background may be ascertained through observation or attention to surnames. How, then, can the interviewer ensure a defense against charges of unlawful discrimination?

The best defense is a sound alternative. That is, if you as an interviewer can point to and explain the basis of your preferences for one applicant over another, *and that basis is clearly job-related,* you are in a strong position. One of the greatest problems in interviewing is the amount of information gathered in the interview that is thrown away in the evaluation process. A distressingly large percentage of interviewers reduce a half hour or more of sound, job-related discussion into a "gut feel" expressed in a few words ("he impressed me") or a series of ratings of highly subjective traits like those seen in the left side of Figure 2.1. Throwing away so much job-related information and evaluating applicants in such highly subjective terms is not only inefficient, but it is also highly risky. Several court cases have been decided in favor of the complainant because selection interviewers evaluated applicants in subjective terms that were not clearly job-related.[14]

The alternative is to rate the applicant in terms of potential to perform specific job responsibilities on the Applicant Evaluation Form shown in Figure 2.2. This type of job-related evaluation is the best defense against claims of discrimination. The more job-related and specific the evaluation, the better the defense.

Data Retention

The third influence of EEO legislation on selection procedures concerns the retention of information on which the selection decision was made. The 1978 Uniform Guidelines on Employee Selection

Procedures require that employers "should maintain and have available for inspection records or other information which will disclose the impact which its tests and other selection procedures have upon employment opportunities of persons by identifiable race, sex, or ethnic group" (Section 4A). Many interviewers record little or nothing after the interview. Others simply jot a few notes on an application form or résumé and toss it into a file. I recommend that Applicant Evaluation Forms be completed by each member of the organization who interviews an applicant, and that these forms be retained for at least six months. Then if challenged to produce proof of nondiscrimination, the employer has good information to fall back on.

The Bottom Line on EEO

What are your chances of being involved in an EEO suit for discrimination in a selection interview? In practical terms, very low. Of over 8,000 federal and state court cases from 1979–1988 that involved discrimination in employment, the selection interview was an issue in only 72 cases.[15] But you need to know enough about EEO to minimize the possibility of charges of discrimination. Furthermore, inappropriate or unlawful questions may not lead to a lawsuit, but they can damage your reputation and the image of your employer. This chapter includes all the guidance you need to ensure that you conduct legal selection interviews.

CONDUCTING THE SELECTION INTERVIEW

Conducting interviews is a skill. Planning them and setting out their content can be learned by following the guidelines already noted, but the result is merely the skeleton of the interview. Adding substance to the skeleton and bringing it to life is a highly developed skill based on sound principles for gathering and probing information. This section presents guidance for conducting selection interviews and illustrates this skill by example.

Preparation for the Interview

Let's just briefly review the steps to be taken to prepare the content of the selection interview. Both you and the applicant have objectives of collecting information, giving information, and checking personal chemistry and corporate culture. A six-point format meets all these objectives. I have also recommended that you list the major responsibilities of the job to be filled and write a number of hypothetical situations. This preparation leads to a semistructured interview that is tailored to a specific job. Awareness of EEO guidelines ensures that you will conduct a lawful interview. Finally, an application form or résumé usually provides a preview of the applicant for you to examine before the interview. The next step is simply to take all this preparation and convert it into a smooth, conversational, effective interview. Let's see how you can do this.

Review the application form or résumé. A cardinal rule of selection interviewing is to review the application form or résumé *before* beginning the interview. If you find yourself in a situation in which applicants arrive with this material in hand, offer them a cup of coffee and ask them to wait for a couple of minutes while you review it.

Review the application form or résumé for several reasons. First, look for something in common with the applicant to use as a rapport builder—a hobby, interest, school, part of the country—that can be used to break the ice at the beginning of the interview. Remember, the rapport-building step is optional; don't force it if you and the applicant have nothing in common.

Next, let's consider any signs that the applicant can do the job. Since the best predictor of future performance is past performance, look first at the previous full- and part-time jobs the applicant has held and identify the one that is *most similar* to the job you are filling. In addition, look for non-work experience, such as extracurricular activities and hobbies, that may involve some of the responsibilities of the job in question. For example, you can probe to find out whether the president of the marketing club planned, organized, and scheduled the work of others. Did the student who held several part-time jobs learn how to plan and organize time and handle stress? Another fertile territory to probe with students is a project in which he or she was required to apply material learned in the classroom. In reviewing previous work and non-work experience, education, and training, you are looking for signs of potential to perform the job responsibilities you will probe in more detail during the interview.

As you review the application form or résumé, look for signs that the applicant will do the job. These are indications of the applicant's interests, preferences, and intentions. You can probe these topics further in the interview to determine why the applicant is applying for this particular job and whether he or she will remain with your organization. As you review the applicant's educational background and work experience, consider the following questions.

1. Is the applicant currently employed?

2. If so, why is the person leaving his or her current job?

3. Why is the applicant interested in your organization?

4. Is a career change involved? Why the change?

5. Is the interviewee applying for a job similar to his or her current job (a lateral move) or one that is a step up in a career progression?

6. How often has the applicant changed jobs in the past? For what reasons?

7. Is the student applying for the type of job that is appropriate for someone with his or her educational background?

As you read the application form or résumé, look for information that raises these questions in your mind, and then plan to probe that information further during the interview. In addition, look for indications of the conditions under which applicants worked that are comparable to those in your organization (e.g., overtime, shift work, travel, pressure, changing priorities) and plan to probe how and how well they dealt with those conditions.

In summary, then, review the applicant on paper with the following goals in mind:

1. Find a rapport builder.

2. Look for signs of past experiences or education that you can probe to assess potential to perform the responsibilities of the job you are filling.

3. Look for signs of interest in the job and your organization and signs of intention to pursue a given career.

Information you will provide the applicant. A major objective of the selection interview is to provide information about the job, organization, and working conditions. How well this is done will affect your organization's image and attractiveness to the applicant. Furthermore, during the interview you are a personification of your organization, and how you conduct yourself may influence the applicant more significantly than all the brochures, annual reports, and organizational charts you can muster. In short, you need to be a professional and appear to have done your homework.

More specifically, interviewers must be armed with information that prospective employees will find useful. In particular it is very helpful for company recruiters who visit university campuses to get together and decide what information is best covered in recruiting brochures and literature and what topics need attention in the interview. Generally, students as well as applicants with more work experience want to learn details of the job for which they are applying. They want to know the job's responsibilities and accountabilities, what a typical day on the job is like, and the kind of people they will be working with. They are also very interested in the organization's opportunities for training and career development. Above all, they want to be told the truth; a hard sell not only runs the risk of alienating some applicants, but it can also increase turnover due to high expectations that are not met.[16]

During the Interview

Even though you have a six-point format, a list of major responsibilities and two or three hypothetical situations, and several points to probe about why the person is applying, you want the interview to appear unplanned and unstructured. The result is a conversational interview in which applicants feel relaxed and conclude that you are genuinely interested in them because you talk so much about topics they raise that are important to them. *The key to a conversational selection interview is to get the applicant to raise many of the topics you want to discuss and then to focus on them.* You can achieve this by following the sequence described in Chapter 1. These steps, when applied to the selection interview, are:

Initiate

Listen

Focus

Probe

Evaluate

We will consider each of these steps and the techniques that they involve shortly but first, let's review the six-point format of the selection interview. The six steps are as follows:

1. Build rapport

2. Set the agenda

3. Gather information

   a. Can the applicant do the job?

   b. Will the applicant do the job?

4. Provide information about the job and organization

5. Answer questions

6. Terminate

Initiate. You will begin by talking about something you have in common with the applicant to build rapport, and then you will set the agenda. At this point you will begin the main portion of the interview by collecting information to determine whether the applicant can do and will do the job. You should begin with the *can do* objective. A good rule of thumb is to begin on the applicant's home territory by finding something the applicant has done that relates to the job you are trying to fill. Initiate the discussion with an open-ended question about a job from the applicant's work history that is most similar to the job that is open. For example,

Initiate

"I see that you are currently working as a process engineer. What are some of your major responsibilities in that job?"

or

"I noticed on your résumé that you spent two summers doing programming for IBM. What kinds of activities were you involved in?"

With students who have no directly related work experience, you can begin with extracurricular activities or class projects and assignments. If you were recruiting for a management trainee, for example, you could begin by asking,

Initiate

"I noticed that you were president of the marketing club. What did that entail?"

or

"I see that you had several organizational behavior courses in your undergraduate business program. What kinds of group projects did you work on?"

Your intention is to get applicants to mention some specific job-related functions they are currently performing or have performed in the past that are similar to the responsibilities of the job you are filling.

Listen. At this point you must simply listen very carefully for topics you wish to pursue. In particular, you will listen for some of the major responsibilities on your list. Careful preparation really pays off here. It stills that little voice in many interviewers' minds that sometimes cries out, "What am I going to say when the applicant stops talking?"

It is important to respond nonverbally to applicants when they are talking. They like to know that the interviewer is alive and well and are sometimes not really sure when they are confronted with a blank face staring back at them. An occasional head nod or "um huh" and leaning forward in the chair shows interest and encourages the applicant to continue talking. In addition, encouraging words, such as "that's interesting" or "that sounds like a fascinating project," are very effective.

Focus and probe. Interviewers do their real work in these two steps. Applicants can (and sometimes do) claim to have any kind of background they want, and the only way you can be sure they are not delivering a rehearsed script or simply lying is to probe. Here's how.

Focus the discussion on topics you want to talk about with a focusing statement, such as "You mentioned..." or "I'm particularly interested in..." You can also focus by paraphrasing a part of what the applicant has just said—"So you spent a lot of time writing code."

Then you begin the following sequence of probes.

HOW?   "How did you write the code?" or "What approach did you take to...?" or "What techniques did you use in...?" or "What was involved in...?"

Always begin probing with a HOW question to learn about the applicant's basic approach to a specific job responsibility.

WHY?   "Why did you do it that way?" or "How did you happen to choose that approach?" or "What was your rationale...?"

The "why" probe is optional because applicants frequently explain why when they answer the "how" question, but use it if you do not understand why the applicant did what he or she claims to have done.

RESULTS?   "What results did you achieve?" or "What feedback did you get?" or "What percentage of your code tested correct on the first trial?" or "How well did that approach work out for you?" or "What was your sales volume?"

You can ask for results in many different ways, depending on the topic. The key is to get applicants to tell you how well they have performed a specific function.

Hypothetical Situation

The hypothetical situation is also *optional*, but you should use it here, *at the bottom of a line of inquiry, only if you feel you still need additional information about how well the applicant will perform this responsibility for your organization.*

Let's put these techniques together in the following example. Suppose you are interviewing a college senior with a computer science major for the position of entry-level programmer in a department in which all projects are done in teams.

INTERVIEWER: "I noticed from your résumé that you spent two summers doing programming for IBM. What kinds of activities were you involved in?"

APPLICANT: "Well, I wrote a lot of code primarily in FORTRAN and COBOL. Generally, we worked in teams under the supervision of a systems analyst. I also prepared documentation and tested the software I wrote."

INTERVIEWER: "You mentioned that you worked in teams. How did you handle your role as a team member?"

APPLICANT: "The systems analyst we were assigned to would call a meeting at the beginning of each new project. I usually tried to participate a lot and volunteer for a particular assignment."

INTERVIEWER: "Why did you take such an active role in the meetings?"

APPLICANT: "Well, I enjoyed the people contact, and also I learned during my first summer that those who spoke up first got their choice of the most interesting assignments."

INTERVIEWER: "That's an interesting strategy. How did it work out for you?"

APPLICANT: "I got most of the assignments I wanted!"

INTERVIEWER: "I see. How did the other team members respond?"

APPLICANT: "I've got to admit that the newer members weren't too happy early in the summer, but then they caught on quickly and everybody became more involved. We had some really lively meetings by the end of the summer."

Notice that the interviewer followed up on points raised by the applicant and probed for more information. We learned quite a bit about how the applicant works in teams and also that the person enjoys people contact, which is an indication of interest and preferences. To learn even more about how the applicant works in a team situation, the interviewer could have used a hypothetical situation at this point in the interview, or asked the applicant to describe other team experiences. Then the interviewer could shift to another topic with a transition, another focusing statement, and a "how" probe.

> "That gives me a good idea of your experience working in teams. Now I'd like to turn to something else you mentioned earlier. You said that you prepared documentation. What approach did you use to documentation?"

Looks pretty easy, doesn't it? Now let's consider a major obstacle. *What if the applicant does not mention all the job responsibilities on your list?* In response to your initial open-ended question, most applicants with related work experience will not list all of the responsibilities of the job you are planning to fill. As in the previous example, you proceed to focus and probe into each responsibility the applicant has mentioned. Then you raise each one not yet discussed with a direct question that can be answered "yes" or "no." Interviewers are usually advised to avoid such questions, but they will not lead to an abrupt halt in the dialogue *if* you know what to ask next.

For example, suppose entry-level computer programmers also meet with users to assess their needs for software. The applicant in the previous illustration didn't say anything about that job responsibility. As the interviewer, you would have to raise that topic by asking, "In your summer job at IBM, did you have any contact with users to assess their needs for the software you wrote?"

1. If the applicant says "yes," you then begin probing with a "how" question.

2. If the applicant says "no," ask whether he or she had any user contact in any other jobs.

3. If the applicant says "yes," then begin probing.

4. If the applicant still says "no," then move into education and training by asking if assessing user needs was ever covered in any of his or her courses.

5. If the applicant says "yes," then probe what was discussed, what he or she learned, how it might be applied, etc.

6. If the applicant still says "no," then you have collected enough information to make an evaluation of potential to perform this responsibility. Since the applicant has never done it before, and has never learned how to do it, you would rate the applicant low.

As an interviewer, you need to continue probing into the applicant's background until you have covered all of the responsibilities of the job you are filling. This will provide all the information you need to evaluate the applicant on section A of the Applicant Evaluation Form in Figure 2.2.

Will do. Next, you need to assess the applicant's willingness to do the job and remain with your organization. Simply discussing the job-related activities the applicant has done before will give you some clues about what he or she likes to do. Here is where your careful listening really pays off. The applicant for the entry-level computer programmer job in the previous example indicated in response to a "why" question that he liked people contact. That is valuable information to probe further.

You can move into "will do" questions with a transition like, "We've talked a lot about the kind of work you've done in the past. Why are you thinking of leaving your current job?" or "What attracted you to this job?" As the discussion about the applicant's preferences continues, you can use the clues you picked up from your discussion of "can do." For example, "You mentioned earlier that you really enjoyed the people contact in your summer jobs at IBM. How much people contact are you looking for in future jobs?" Additional questions about the applicant's long-term career goals are also useful. These questions are sometimes anticipated by coached applicants, who have prepared answers. But questions appear far less "canned" if they follow 20 minutes of conversational probing about the applicant's previous work experience and education.

Finally, in probing applicants' preferences and intentions, remember to inquire about the conditions under which they have worked. Suppose the computer programmer job to be filled in the previous example involves at least ten hours of overtime a week. The interviewer would probe applicant's exposure to and feelings about prospective overtime in the following way:

INTERVIEWER: "In your two summer jobs at IBM, how much overtime did you work?"

APPLICANT: "Almost none."

INTERVIEWER: "Have you worked overtime in any of your previous jobs?"

APPLICANT: "I used to work weekends in a grocery store, and the manager was always asking us to stay late on Saturday and Sunday nights to clean up."

INTERVIEWER: "How often did you stay late?"

APPLICANT: "Quite a bit."

INTERVIEWER: "You don't sound very happy about that." (The interviewer is reflecting a feeling, as discussed in Chapter 1.)

APPLICANT: "I wasn't very happy. I had to break a lot of dates because of that job."

INTERVIEWER: "So you stayed late pretty often." (The interviewer paraphrases the applicant's response.)

APPLICANT: "Yes, somebody had to, and I needed the money."

INTERVIEWER: "How would you feel about working overtime in this job?"

APPLICANT: "I'm willing to do what is necessary to get the work done. I have several friends currently working in the computer field, and they have told me that overtime is a fact of life. I figure it comes with the territory."

INTERVIEWER: "So you have an idea of what to expect. Would you be available to work at least ten hours of overtime per week?" (Notice that the question is in *job-related* terms to avoid any EEO problems. Questions about marital status, children, or child care are unlawful.)

APPLICANT: "Yes, as long as I had a day's notice to plan for it."

INTERVIEWER: "That's certainly a reasonable request."

It takes a lot of skill and practice to conduct selection interviews with a conversational tone. Many interviewers rely too heavily on the question, and this can cause the interview to take on the question-answer, question-answer, question-answer flavor of an interrogation. This type of interview does little to attract the applicant to you and your organization. On the other hand, heavy reliance on the nondirective techniques discussed in Chapter 1 can be very annoying. Wagging your head for 20 minutes and muttering "um huh" won't do you much good, and overindulgence in paraphrasing ideas and reflecting feelings may make the applicant wonder if there is an echo in the interview room. Try for a mixture of specific probes and nondirective techniques. Skillful interviewers are able to use the appropriate technique at the right time to meet their objectives.

Additional Reminders

Eye contact, body language, and voice. Have you ever noticed how seldom people actually look at one another when they are speaking? Many of us look off somewhere, and then, when we finish our question or answer, we swing our eyes back to the other person. Look your applicants in the eye when you are talking with them! This can be overdone, of course, but direct eye contact and using the applicant's name makes the interview more personal.

Be aware of your body position and voice. One of your worst enemies is fatigue or lack of interest, both of which show up in posture and voice. A monotone delivery of information about the job and company can be deadly. As a representative of your organization, you are performing during the interview and you must work hard to keep your energy level high. If you are interested in what the applicant has just said, allow yourself to lean forward and let the pitch and volume of your voice rise. If you are bored, struggle not to show it. Picture yourself late one afternoon, slouched in your chair, looking into space, and saying in a weak monotone, "I'm really impressed with your résumé; you're just the kind of person we're looking for." This just won't work. What you say means far less than how you say it.

Leading questions, supplying the answer, or multiple questions. It is surprising to realize how much of our own opinions or ideas we communicate in the way we phrase our questions. Consider the following examples:

> "You have had supervisory experience, haven't you?"
> "You wouldn't have any problem with overtime, would you?"
> "When you are assigned a project, do you prefer to plan your own approach, or do you like your supervisor to tell you how to proceed?"

These are called leading questions because they suggest an answer. To do well, applicants can simply say yes to the first two and choose the more desirable first option in the multiple-choice question. Some of us even ask and answer our own questions. For example, an interviewer may say, "How did you become interested in manufacturing? You mentioned earlier that your father was a plant manager for 25 years; that was probably a major influence, wasn't it?" This type of question gives the applicant a chance to lean back, relax, and think, "Keep it up, you're doing great." For a good illustration of this questioning technique, just tune in any TV talk show and listen carefully to how the host directs the conversation by asking leading questions or answering his or her own questions.

Another common fault is for the interviewer to ask a series of questions before allowing the applicant a chance to respond. For example,

> INTERVIEWER: "When confronted with a problem, what approach do you take to problem solving? Do you try to find a solution yourself or ask for help? How effective have you been?"

> APPLICANT: "I think I've been very successful in solving the problems I've faced."

Here the interviewer should have stopped with the first question, which is an excellent "how" probe. The second question leads the applicant by providing two alternatives, and the third is a "how well" probe. Notice that the applicant answered the last question, which is quite common. The general rule is to ask the first question and then sit back and listen. Then probe the applicant's response for more detail.

GUIDE FOR GATHERING INFORMATION

We have discussed how interviewers can initiate, listen, focus, and probe to learn whether applicants can and will perform the job. Before we deal with the last step—evaluate—we need to consider how the information can be collected and used as efficiently as possible. We know that work and non-work experience, training, and education are the territories we must probe to assess the applicant's potential to perform the job. It is in these areas that interviewers discover the job responsibilities that the applicant has either done or learned how to do in the past. How interviewers collect this information is a crucial issue in conducting the interview.

Avoid following the résumé as a guide. Most interviewers use the résumé or application form as a guide for gathering information in phase 3 of the overall format of the selection interview.

During the interview they work through the résumé or application form section by section, probing into education, work experience, extracurricular activities, and so on. Then, after the interview is over, they scratch their heads and try to recall what the applicant said about each major responsibility of the job they are filling.

Following the résumé as the primary guide during the interview is relatively unfocused and inefficient. There is an easier way. Let's review what we know about the human frailties of interviewers. They forget, form first impressions and jump to conclusions, make unsupported inferences, and selectively distort and ignore information. If interviewers follow the résumé as a guide and probe into all the applicant's previous work and non-work experience, training, and education, these human frailties can and do still operate. Interviewers forget. They form a favorable first impression and therefore minimize the applicant's lack of experience in, for example, documentation. They forget to work systematically through the how, why, and results probes and fail to find out about the applicant's method of supervision in a previous job. After the interview is over and they are rating the applicant, they may find themselves hampered because they have forgotten or distorted some information and have neglected to cover other relevant topics. How often have you felt exasperated after an interview because you forgot to ask the applicant something important?

Job responsibilities as a guide. In examining an applicant's potential to perform the job, interviewers need a format that helps them probe systematically into all relevant topics in spite of human frailties. That format is based on the major responsibilities that make up the job to be filled. Rather than working through the résumé globally, interviewers need to cover the past in a more focused way. If ten major responsibilities have been identified for the job, the interviewer needs to probe into the applicant's past ten times, each time focusing on one of the major responsibilities. Although you might think this procedure appears stilted, with practice it can be done as a smooth conversation with no apparent structure, as illustrated in the earlier examples of the initiate, listen, focus, and probe techniques.

One last point. Do not feel that you have to discuss every item on the résumé or application form. As was already noted, the best predictor of future performance is past performance. Therefore, you need to begin with previous work or non-work experience by probing into the most clearly related previous job, regardless of where it appears on the résumé or application form. And don't feel you have to discuss every job in the work history. Probe previous work experience only until you have covered all of the major job responsibilities. Furthermore, probe into education and training only if the applicant has not performed a specific job responsibility before. What territory you probe, and how much, depends on what that applicant has to offer.

After the interview. If you probe in a focused way only into the part of the applicant's background that is related to potential and willingness to do the job you are filling, then evaluating the applicant is relatively straightforward. First, every member of the organization involved in the selection process should identify the major responsibilities of the job to be filled and enter them in Section A of the Applicant Evaluation Form in Figure 2.2. Then *immediately after* finishing the interview, each interviewer should independently complete all the ratings on the form. Finally, all interviewers can compare and discuss their ratings and come to a group decision.

In considering the evaluations on the form, you should place primary emphasis on Section A; the decision to hire or reject an applicant must be based mainly on interviewer assessments of his or her potential to perform the job effectively. Judgments of the applicant's interest and commitment in Section B are less important, but they should be considered, especially for jobs that suffer high levels of turnover. Section C contains highly subjective impressions of the applicant that should be used when a group of interviewers is forced to choose among several well-qualified applicants who were evaluated about the same in Sections A and B.

All these evaluations are subjective and can therefore be challenged for personal bias or discrimination. There is simply no way to eliminate all the subjectivity from the evaluation of job applicants, but here are two key recommendations for reducing subjectivity. First, as has been stressed already, you need to evaluate applicants in job-related terms; specifically in terms of their potential to perform the job responsibilities in Section A of the Applicant Evaluation Form. These evaluations are far less subjective than ratings of ambiguous traits like attitude, maturity, aggressiveness, and initiative. Second, you must probe into what applicants tell you they have done and learned in the past. In fact, applicants can distort their work record (and some do) and can claim on a résumé or application form to have held any job. They can also claim in the interview to have performed any responsibility, whether they did so or not. The secret to cutting through the distortions is to ask follow-up questions about "how, why, and results achieved." Few applicants can bluff their way through such detailed probing.

POTENTIAL PROBLEMS

So far, we have stressed a *job-related* approach to selection interviewing, in terms of preparing for the interview, probing for information during the interview, and evaluating applicants after the interview. But many interviewers face situations in which this approach may not seem feasible. Let's discuss how you can handle these types of situations.

What if the interview is not for a specific job? There are many instances in which you may not be interviewing for a specific job. This often occurs in recruiting interviews on college campuses. Human resource specialists also face this situation when recruiting for a general category of positions, like clerical jobs or semi-skilled factory jobs. Confronted with this situation, interviewers often resort to the psychiatric approach in Figure 2.1 and simply assess applicants in terms of personal traits.

There is a better option. Frequently in campus recruiting, interviewers may not be interviewing for a specific job, but they are screening for a family of jobs in a particular functional area. For example, recruiters of engineering students may be screening for entry-level engineering positions in a number of different departments. Similarly, a human resource specialist may be screening for factory positions ranging from material handler to assembler to machine operator. It is often possible to group these jobs into *families* of jobs with common responsibilities. All recruiters should identify the major responsibilities common to all jobs in the family and enter them in Section A of the Applicant Evaluation Form in Figure 2.2. For example, all the engineering jobs might involve collecting and analyzing data, preparing reports, presenting those reports to co-workers and management, working in a team, directing the work of technical assistants, and planning and organizing one's own time and work. Recruiters could then probe each student's experience and training in these activities and evaluate his or her potential to perform them. Whether an applicant is more suitable for one job or another in the family would then depend on his or her level of potential to perform the job responsibilities.

What if the interview is not for a family of jobs? Some interviewers, usually human resource specialists, find themselves facing applicants when there is no specific job to be filled. This sometimes happens when applicants simply walk in to the human resource department or when a member of an organization interviews a person as a favor to someone else. This is a difficult interview to conduct because you are essentially working in a vacuum, but you can still avoid simply assessing the applicant in terms of personal traits. In this situation you are not really conducting a selection interview; you are conducting an examination of what the applicant can do and wants to do. Simply study the application form or résumé and find the applicant's most recent job, and then during the interview use the initiate, listen, focus, and probe technique to probe how well the applicant has performed specific job responsibilities that he or she mentions. Also probe into preferences, interests, and career goals. Then you can decide whether there is a position in your organization for this person.

Team Interviewing

As employers share power with employees through participative management and self-managed work teams, many employees now take part in decisions previously reserved for managers and supervisors. The growing emphasis on teamwork is especially evident in selection interviewing as team members interview job applicants and make hiring recommendations. Team interviewing requires careful planning before the interview and skilled coordination during the interview.

Before the interview. As discussed earlier in this chapter, planning for a selection interview should begin with a clear description of the position to be filled. Therefore, all members of a team should identify the job's major responsibilities and place them in Section A of the Applicant Evaluation Form in Figure 2.2. This step ensures that all interviewers cover the same content and assess applicants with the same standards.

During the interview. Team interviews can be conducted in two ways: *sequential* or *group*. In the sequential approach, each team member conducts an individual interview with the applicant by following the procedures already discussed in this chapter. However, problems can occur when an applicant is interviewed by too many people. For example, some employers schedule job applicants for interviews with as many as eight team members during a day. If each interviewer conducts a highly structured interview with the same prepared questions, the day can appear repetitive and grueling to the applicant. The semistructured, flexible approach recommended in this chapter is especially important to maintain a balance between the objectives of collecting information from applicants and attracting them to the organization because it allows each interview to appear like an unplanned conversation.

In the group approach, two or more team members interview the applicant at the same time. This approach reduces the number of interviews applicants must undergo, but it greatly increases the need for coordination among members of the interviewing team and also places more stress on the applicant. Applicants who face a panel of ten interviewers may feel like they have been through an inquisition rather than a selection process. Furthermore, team interviews almost always appear disorganized and unprofessional to applicants because the topic under discussion continually shifts as different team members ask questions on different subjects.

Interviewing teams can conduct well-organized, coordinated conversations with applicants by appointing a leader to direct team members through the interview format and by following the initiate, listen, focus, probe sequence discussed earlier in this chapter. The team leader should initiate the interview by introducing the team members, building rapport with the applicant, setting the agenda, and asking an open-ended question about a related job which the applicant has held. The leader then focuses on one of the job's major responsibilities (identified by the team before the interview), and team members ask "how," "why," and "results" probes. The leader then focuses on the other major responsibilities in turn, and team members follow up with probing questions. The team leader continues through the remainder of the format, and team members add necessary questions or comments. Interviewing teams can use this approach very effectively to conduct selection interviews in an organized fashion and still involve all team members in a conversational way.

After the interview. It is important that members of interviewing teams independently assess each applicant immediately after completing the interview. They should record their judgments on the Applicant Evaluation Form and then meet to discuss differences between their evaluations and eventually to reach a group decision on each applicant.

THE BOTTOM LINE

Now that I have covered extensively how you can plan the content of selection interviews and conduct them efficiently, one question remains: "Will it work?" The bottom line on the selection interview is whether it is effective; that is, reliable and valid. It is up to you to examine your interviews to assess their reliability and predictive validity.

Reliability. Assessing reliability is straightforward if you have designed the interview carefully and have identified the major responsibilities on which applicants are to be evaluated. Let's say that over the course of six months you interview 25 applicants who are also seen by one or more other members of your organization. Compare your evaluations of each applicant in Section A of the Applicant Evaluation Form, responsibility by responsibility, with the evaluations made by other interviewers. Check to see if the ratings are similar, differing by only a point on the five-point scale. The more consistent the ratings, the more reliable the interview. It is also possible to have a human resource specialist compute correlation coefficients to place a numerical value on the estimate of reliability. Anyone who interviews applicants who are also interviewed by someone else can assess reliability.

Validity. The first step to validity is reliability. That is, a selection device that is not reliable cannot predict performance accurately. If you have evidence of reliability, your next step is to determine whether your assessments of applicants' potential to perform are related to their actual performance as new employees.

Assessing validity is not nearly as straightforward as testing reliability, and there are a number of methods for doing so.[17] I recommend that anyone who conducts selection interviews regularly perform a crude test of validity. To do so, you need to retain your evaluations of applicants (this is advisable for EEO purposes

Figure 2.3
VALIDATING THE SELECTION INTERVIEW

	Marginal (20)	High (55)
High (35)	5	30
Moderate (30)	8	22
Low (10)	7	3

Performance

Interview Assessments

anyway), and you need to collect some measure of performance of the applicants who were hired. Here is the first practical problem in assessing validity. While you can measure the performance of those applicants you hire, you will never know how well those you rejected would have performed. You are therefore working with limited information. Let's proceed, though, and see what you can learn even from limited information.

Let's consider a situation in which 75 applicants were interviewed and hired. After they have been employed for at least six months, collect their performance appraisal forms and group them into three categories of performance: high, moderate, and low. In the example shown in Figure 2.3, 35 are performing in the high category, 30 are in the moderate category, and ten are low. Next consult your interview records and summarize your assessments of each applicant's potential to perform as either high or marginal. In our example, 55 fell into the high category and 20 were marginal. Now you simply assign employees to the areas in the figure according to the categories into which they fall. Of the 20 marginal applicants, seven are currently low performers, eight are moderate, and only five are high. Of the 55 applicants rated high, 30 are performing well, 22 moderately, and only three are low. This crude test demonstrates a good level of predictive validity. Human resource specialists can use larger numbers of applicants to compute a more sophisticated correlational analysis of validity for the entire organization.

It is important that organizations examine the validity of the interview, along with all other selection devices. Only then can you interview applicants and know not only how effective you are, but also how strong your evidence is against claims of discrimination.

Performance Appraisal Interviewing

3

"What a disappointment that was! I went into my supervisor's office expecting to discuss my job performance and developmental goals, but he did all the talking. Then he just handed me the evaluation form and told me to sign it."

"These rating forms are impossible. Why does the personnel department want me to do a personality analysis of my staff at appraisal time?"

"Man, was that frustrating. I wanted to hear Johnson's views of her own job performance and her ideas for work goals, but all she wanted to talk about was how large her salary increase would be next year."

"I had such high hopes for that interview, but it was so awkward and unnatural that we never did get into a fruitful discussion."

The performance appraisal interview probably requires more skill from the supervisor or manager than does any other interview covered in this book. Supervisors who have a good day-to-day relationship with their employees often see that relationship severely strained during the annual, formal interview that is often awkward and even painful for both parties. Whether on the giving or receiving end of these interviews, many employees report extreme reactions to them. A poorly handled performance appraisal interview can depress a supervisor, crush an employee's morale, and send that employee directly to the help wanted or career section of the newspaper. On the other hand, an effective appraisal interview can be an exhilarating and motivating experience for both the supervisor and the employee.

Unfortunately, problems in performance appraisal interviews have become so common that human resource specialists in organizations with formal appraisal systems report extreme difficulty in getting supervisors and managers even to conduct these interviews. Recent surveys have documented the problems encountered when supervisors formally assess and discuss the performance of their employees.[1] One found that over 70% of employees of 200 large companies reported that they were more confused than enlightened by the performance appraisal feedback they received. Another survey of 3,500 companies reported that the organization's performance appraisal system was the most frequently mentioned human resource concern. Still another survey conducted by the American Society of Personnel Administration (now the Society for Human Resource Management) concluded that less than 10% of performance appraisal systems are "reasonably successful."

The performance appraisal interview is a discussion between an employee and his or her immediate supervisor which focuses on that employee's job performance over the past year and includes some planning for changes in future performance. Employers may refer to this type of interview with a variety of terms, such as performance review, work planning and review, or performance evaluation, all of which have basically the same meaning. Most organizations with over several hundred employees have a *formal* performance appraisal system, consisting of rating forms that supervisors fill out at least once a year, followed by a discussion with the employee. In smaller organizations, the assessment of each employer's performance may take place more *informally* (there are often no official rating forms), but supervisors usually assess an employee's performance about the same time that they make decisions about salary increases.

This interview differs in two basic ways from the day-to-day feedback, coaching, and planning that occurs between a supervisor and employee. First, it takes a longer look into both the past and the future by considering the employee's job performance for the entire past year and making plans for the next year. Second, whereas day-to-day feedback usually deals with a narrow range of the employee's performance (a specific project or job responsibility), the performance appraisal interview focuses on a broader range—all aspects of the employee's job performance. Performance appraisal interviews occur annually in most organizations and as often as quarterly in some.

These interviews certainly affect all working people significantly—in our pocketbooks and in the pride we take in our accomplishments at work. If we feel that we have been dealt with unfairly or insensitively in either of these areas, we are likely to feel very dissatisfied. This places added pressure on supervisors and managers to conduct skillful appraisal interviews. It is very unfortunate, however, that so few receive any training in how to conduct these interviews. This is not a skill that many bosses can afford to pick up by trial and error. The trials are very trying, and the errors are exceedingly costly.

OBJECTIVES

Let's begin at the beginning. As with all the interviews in this book, the performance appraisal interview has several objectives that must be carefully addressed if the interview is to succeed. The objectives fall into two general categories.

Develop employees and improve their performance. One major purpose of performance appraisal is to help employees do a better job. This purpose includes several specific objectives, which are:

1. To clarify the employee's job responsibilities, work goals, and performance standards to be achieved.

2. To discuss the employee's level of job performance.

3. To promote the development of employees by identifying training needs and counseling, as well as coaching and motivating employees to improve their performance.

4. To discuss the employee's views of the causes of his or her job performance and suggestions for improvement.

5. To establish mutual work goals.

6. To promote career development by discussing long-range plans for development and promotion.

Each of these objectives helps your employees do a better job and, therefore, helps you perform more effectively. As a manager or supervisor, you need to ensure that your employees understand what they are supposed to do and the performance standards they are expected to achieve. Input from employees is important here because they are often more familiar with the shifting priorities of their job responsibilities and projects than you may be.

Another major objective is to evaluate your employees' performance before the interview and provide feedback and discuss their performance during the interview. Feedback takes a variety of forms. For example, in some organizations a supervisor and an employee review goals set during the last performance appraisal interview and base evaluations on how well the goals were met. In other companies, supervisors fill out a rating form that is the basis for the feedback given to employees.

To meet the third and fourth objectives, you and your employees must identify the *causes* of their performance. Do they need additional training to increase their levels of skill and knowledge required to do the job? Do they need more direction and feedback from you? Are they unmotivated? Did factors outside their control prevent them from reaching their goals? Here you are learning as much as possible from your employees so you can take whatever action is needed to ensure that they will maintain or improve their level of performance in the future.

In the performance appraisal interview, you also need to look toward the future. You and your employees may set work goals to be met during the next year. You may also discuss longer-range plans to help identify developmental opportunities and chart their careers over a number of years.

I want to emphasize that two-way communication is important for the successful achievement of all six objectives just discussed. Insights from employees are often crucial to their own development and improved performance. To help your employees do a better job, therefore, you must assume the role of *listener and counselor.*

Communicate and support administrative decisions. The second general category includes an objective of the performance appraisal interview that is often uppermost in an employee's mind at appraisal time—"How much more will I be paid next year? How about that promotion?" The performance appraisal interview provides a vehicle through which you, as an immediate supervisor, pass along decisions based on employee performance (e.g., salary increases, promotions, and transfers) to your employees. Since a supervisor's appraisal of employee performance usually strongly affects these decisions, you may need not only to communicate these decisions but also to justify or even defend them by revealing your evaluations of the employee's performance during the interview. This objective places managers and supervisors in the role of judge; many feel as if they are grading and talking down to their employees, as a parent would talk to a child.

IMPROVING THE PERFORMANCE APPRAISAL INTERVIEW

As already mentioned, conducting performance appraisal interviews may be the most difficult assignment you are asked to carry out as a manager or supervisor.[2] There are three basic reasons for this difficulty, summarized in Table 3.1. First, you have *several objectives* in the performance appraisal interview, and you will have to plan carefully to meet all those objectives effectively.

Second, every objective in the interview depends on the measures and procedures used to appraise employee performance. You enter the interview with an appraisal in your head or on paper. It is the basis for your salary and promotional recommendations. Your discussion of employee performance also draws heavily from your formal or informal appraisal of his or her

Table 3.1
WEAKNESSES OF THE PERFORMANCE APPRAISAL INTERVIEW

I.   Multiple Objectives

    A.   Conflict between performance improvement/employee development and administrative decisions

    B.   Objectives require the interviewer to assume multiple roles

    C.   Not all objectives apply to all employees

II.   Methods Used to Appraise Employee Performance

    A.   Many appraisal methods are highly subjective

    B.   Appraisal methods may violate EEO standards

    C.   Feedback is not useful to the employee

III.   Approach to the Interview

    A.   Supervisors do not have a well-considered approach

    B.   Different approaches work with different employees

performance. Any plans that you and your employee make for the future will be based on your appraisal of that employee. In many cases, however, the method a supervisor used to appraise performance before entering the interview is highly subjective and unclear to the employee and is therefore open to challenge. If the appraisal method is flawed, chances are very high that you will have trouble meeting all your objectives in the interview.

Third, how you approach the performance appraisal interview is crucial. The appropriate approach is seldom intuitively obvious, and the skills in conducting a successful interview with a given approach are very difficult to learn by trial and error. You need to develop these skills carefully in order to conduct performance appraisal interviews effectively. Let's take a closer look at the three reasons for failure in the performance appraisal interview and see what you can do to minimize or avoid them. Steps you can take to improve your performance appraisal interviews are listed in Table 3.2.

Multiple objectives. As in all interviews, you have much to achieve in the performance appraisal interview. The major objectives require you to assume two quite different roles during the interview. In one role you are primarily *giving information* to your employees. You have to do a good deal of talking and telling as you give them feedback on their performance and communicate administrative decisions. As you hear an employee's assessment of his or her own performance, explore the causes of employee performance, set mutual work goals, and discuss career plans, you assume a more passive role of *seeking information* and listening. These two roles of acting as an authority figure who delivers information but also as a consultant who listens and counsels are quite different from one another and require considerable skill from the interviewer.

Furthermore, there is some inherent conflict within the set of objectives. Communicating and supporting administrative decisions tends to take precedence over improving performance and developing employees.[3] In many cases, as soon as the discussion turns to the percentage of salary increase or the denial of a

Table 3.2
IMPROVING THE PERFORMANCE APPRAISAL INTERVIEW

I.   Planning the Interview to Meet Specific Objectives

    A.   Split performance improvement/employee development and administrative decisions into two interviews

    B.   Plan an interview format to meet specific objectives

    C.   Tailor interview objectives to the employee

II.   Methods Used to Appraise Employee Performance

    A.   Evaluate performance and results, not personal traits and skills

    B.   Ensure that the appraisal method meets EEO standards

    C.   Make feedback useful to employees

III.   Approach to the Interview

    A.   Plan an approach that meets your objectives

    B.   Tailor your approach to the employee and your own supervisory style

---

desired promotion, goal setting and upward communication are lost in the shuffle. If the employee is unhappy with the raise, he or she may ask you to justify the decision. At this point you may present the appraisal in defense of the administrative decision, and the employee may counterattack. The discussion can degenerate into a rather heated debate in which little actual listening occurs but instead each party becomes intent on scoring points. This atmosphere is hardly conducive to a positive discussion of performance improvement and employee development.

Planning the interview to meet specific objectives. This conflict in objectives has prompted the recommendation that the two general categories of objectives—performance improvement/employee development and administrative decisions—be addressed in two separate interviews.[4] Some writers[5] disagree with this recommendation, however, on the basis of surveys that indicate that employees want to discuss both topics in performance appraisal interviews.

Let's look more closely at the two categories of objectives and see if we can resolve these different opinions and come up with some practical guidelines. The vast majority of managers and supervisors conduct performance appraisal interviews *once a year*. Why? Because employers set budgets and make decisions on salary increases and promotions once a year, and every member of the organization knows when it's "that time of year." If a supervisor or manager conducts annual performance appraisal interviews, employees quite naturally expect salary to be discussed. But how often should employees and bosses meet to discuss plans to improve performance and develop employees? Just like taking a bath—as often as necessary. With inexperienced employees, quarterly discussions may be needed. In many project-oriented organizations, supervisors review employee performance at the completion of each project. Finally, annual performance reviews may be sufficient for employees who have done the same job for many years.

Supervisors and managers should conduct interviews primarily to improve performance and develop employees *as often as necessary* for the benefit of both parties and the organization as a whole. In addition, I recommend annual salary review interviews to sum up the year's performance and discuss administrative decisions based on employee performance. For organizations in which supervisors want to conduct both interviews only once, I advise against combining the two. Instead, annual interviews for performance improvement and employee development should be conducted in an organization one or two months *before* salary budgets are set for the upcoming year. When each department receives its final budget and salary increases are determined, then a second set of interviews can be conducted to communicate and support administrative decisions. This approach helps the supervisor and employee concentrate primarily on one set of objectives in each interview, and it also discourages the widespread practice of supervisors' working backward (i.e., deciding on a merit increase and then appraising employee performance to justify the increase). In 20 years of consulting in performance appraisal, I have seen many firms successfully adopt this approach of focusing the interview primarily on either performance improvement/employee development or administrative decisions. Therefore, the remainder of this chapter focuses on the performance appraisal interview dealing primarily with improving performance and developing employees.

One more point on objectives. Before you conduct a performance appraisal interview, you should review the six objectives under performance improvement/employee development and determine which are appropriate for a given employee. For new, career-oriented employees all six may apply. They are eager to discuss their performance and receive supervisory feedback, and they are also very interested in discussing how they can improve and in pursuing opportunities for training and development. But not every employee is on the "fast track" to promotion. What about the reliable, above-average performers who have risen to their level in the organization and are going no further? With these employees, you may wish to scale down the interview to discussing their performance and setting work goals for the next year. It is important that you have a clear plan for which objectives are most suitable for each employee you interview.

Measures of employee performance. Your success or failure in the interview certainly depends heavily on how you evaluate employee performance. All six objectives which contribute to performance improvement and employee development build on an organization's appraisal of employee performance. Poor methods and procedures for appraising performance are often overlooked as a major cause of failure in performance appraisal interviews.

Condensing an employee's performance over a period of six months or one year into a relatively concise and meaningful appraisal is difficult. The tools you have to work with strongly influence the accuracy and quality of your appraisals. Unfortunately, the appraisal tools of most organizations simply aren't very good. Most are highly subjective, whether they're a set of rating scales, or judgments about how well an employee met a goal. Of course, there is no way to eliminate all of the subjectivity from performance appraisal, but some procedures are better than others. Let's have a look at some common appraisal methods, shown in Table 3.3. They are divided into three categories.[6] The first category includes evaluations of employees' personal traits and skills, or *what they are or have*. The second focuses on assessments of employees' performance, or *what they do*. The third consists of employees' results, or *what they achieve*.

Evaluating personal traits and skills. Most appraisal methods evaluate *people* rather than what they do or achieve. The rating scale is the most common tool used for the subjective evaluation of employee performance. Rating scales come in many sizes and shapes, but they are typically headed by the characteristic being rated (e.g., initiative, cooperativeness, attitude, interpersonal skill,

Table 3.3
PERFORMANCE APPRAISAL METHODS

	I	II	III
Information Collected	Traits and Skills (What employee is or has)	Performance (What employee does)	Results (What employee achieves)
Appraisal Method	1. Trait rating scales	1. Essay appraisals	1. Management by objectives
	2. Assessments of employee skills	2. Behavioral checklists	2. Work planning and review
		3. Behaviorally based rating scales	

Table 3.4
TYPICAL RATING SCALE

INITIATIVE

5	Exceptional
4	Better than average
3	Usually meets the situation
2	Easily discouraged by obstacles
1	Poor

---

maturity). Along the continuum of the scale are numbers and phrases to identify different levels of the characteristic under scrutiny (e.g., excellent, average, consistently exceeds requirements). An example of a typical rating scale is given in Table 3.4.

Major problems occur when rating scales are used to evaluate employees' personal traits and skills. First, the personal characteristics are not clearly defined. Quite simply, the employee and supervisor do not know what they're talking about when they discuss ratings of traits and skills in a performance appraisal interview. Consider the case in which the supervisor has rated an employee on initiative, using the rating scale in Table 3.4.

SUPERVISOR: "And on initiative I rated you at the '3' level, which is average. I feel that you have room for improvement in this area."

EMPLOYEE: "What do you mean by initiative?"

SUPERVISOR: "Well, you know what initiative is; it's a kind of get-up-and-go, take-charge attitude toward your work."

EMPLOYEE: "You mean I'm not motivated?"

SUPERVISOR: "Well no, not exactly. You're motivated, but initiative goes beyond that. You need to be a self-starter."

EMPLOYEE: "What's a self-starter?"

SUPERVISOR: "Well..."

Have you ever been on the giving or receiving end of such a conversation? It can make you feel pretty confused. Does your organization have rating scales that require you to make judgments about the basic character of employees? These rating scales thrust you directly into the role of judge of the employee's character—you are providing employees with feedback about what they are and have rather than what they do. The employee becomes confused or defensive and the interview degenerates.

In some organizations, appraisals are done more informally. The supervisor may consider an employee's performance over the past year and then write out the employee's strong and weak points in a narrative. Unfortunately, these narratives are often written in terms of basic personal characteristics and, therefore, suffer from the same problems as rating scales of traits and skills.

Another major weakness of appraisal methods which evaluate traits and skills is that they force supervisors to assess employees on characteristics *that are not directly observed*. Supervisors do not see initiative or attitude or maturity or even job knowledge and interpersonal skill, but instead they see a large number of individual behaviors from which they have to *infer* these traits and skills. Of course, if you and I define the trait or skill differently, depending on our own personal experience, and if you fill out a rating scale on me, we will differ in our views of whether the ratings truly reflect how well I have performed. That leads to real trouble in the interview.

Performance appraisal and the law. Evaluations of personal characteristics, regardless of the method used, are totally inappropriate in performance appraisal. These methods make supervisors and managers "play God" and judge employees in vague abstractions. These evaluations result in poor communication and defensiveness in the performance appraisal interview. Furthermore, highly subjective appraisal methods open organizations up to charges of discrimination against protected groups of employees (women and minorities).

As you may know, Title VII of the Civil Rights Act of 1964 prohibits discrimination in terms, conditions, and privileges of employment, and the 1978 Uniform Guidelines of Employee Selection Procedures clearly specify that EEO legislation applies to employment decisions such as "promotion, demotion, retention, and transfer... and other decisions (that) lead to any of the decisions listed above."[7] In short, any formal or informal assessment of employee performance that affects salary, retention, and promotion decisions concerning current employees is subject to EEO legislation.[8] For example, in the case of *Rowe v. General Motors Corporation*, the Court of Appeals for the Fifth Circuit ruled that blacks had been unfairly denied promotions and transfers because the performance appraisal on which the promotions and transfers were based was subjective and vague. Any manager or supervisor can be charged with unlawful discrimination by an employee of a protected class who feels he or she was denied a raise or promotion on the basis of factors unrelated to performance. For example, a woman can charge that a male supervisor rated her low on maturity because of a personal bias against women. A disabled employee can claim that a low rating on motivation was based on a stereotype about disabled people. Appraisal methods that evaluate poorly defined personal traits and skills that are not directly observed are wide open to charges of discrimination.

A recent federal appeals ruling[9] underscored another legal risk of poor performance appraisal practices. Many supervisors and managers evaluate employee performance more favorably than it actually deserves to avoid unpleasant confrontations with their employees. This practice not only distorts the feedback employees receive, but it also postpones the inevitable need to face directly and honestly the responsibility of helping those employees improve their performance or placing them in another job. Managers of a major employer pursued this practice with a black employee, who had been one of the department's best performers in the past but whose performance had slipped in recent years. The manager avoided confronting the employee with accurate evaluations of her performance because the company wanted to avoid charges of racial discrimination. When the company decided to cut costs by dismissing poor performers in the department, however, the employee was surprised to find herself among those who were fired. She successfully sued the company on the grounds that, because she was black, she had not received accurate performance appraisals or the opportunity to improve her performance.

APPRAISING PERFORMANCE AND RESULTS

How can an organization avoid the risks inherent in evaluating employee traits and skills? There are other approaches to performance appraisal that still involve some subjectivity, but are far more *job-related* and provide a much sounder basis for the performance appraisal interview. They appear in columns II and III of Table 3.3. Let's consider each.

Evaluating performance. Employees should be evaluated in terms of *what they do, not what they are or have.* Appraisal methods that truly evaluate the performance of employees provide an appropriate basis for performance appraisal interviews. Three common methods for evaluating performance are listed in Table 3.3. Essay appraisals are most common in small organizations where the performance appraisal process is rather informal. Supervisors or managers summarize in narrative form the major responsibilities of an employee and how well he or she has performed these responsibilities. Essay appraisals are most likely to focus on performance (rather than on personal traits and skills) when they are based on a job description that lists the main duties of the job.

Behavioral checklists are more standardized than are essay appraisals. These checklists may include between a few dozen to over a hundred specific duties for which employees are responsible, as well as undesirable behaviors. The supervisor or manager then checks each duty that the employee has performed satisfactorily, or records how often the employee performed each duty and undesirable behavior, and a total score is computed to reflect the level of performance of each employee.

Behaviorally based rating scales[10] are another example of performance appraisals. They are essentially an extension of behavioral checklists. That is, specific examples of performance are placed along the continuum of a rating scale, depending on how positive or negative those examples are. In Table 3.5, specific examples of the responsibility being rated—for example, *communicating*—appear next to points on the rating scale. If you compare the rating scales in Tables 3.4 and 3.5, you will find that the behaviorally based scale is superior to the trait-rating scale in three ways. First, the factor that is being evaluated is *behavioral.* The act of communicating can be directly observed rather than inferred, as is the case with a trait such as initiative. Second, the factor being evaluated is defined to minimize the possibility of different interpretations by supervisors. Third, the points on the scale, rather than being defined by vague terms like "good" or "exceeds minimal requirements," are defined by actual examples of on-the-job performance. This makes the rating scales easier for the supervisor or manager to fill out and easier for the employee to understand in a feedback session.[11]

Evaluating results. Another common procedure for appraising employee performance is to assess the quality of results employees produce. The performance appraisal interview focuses on the review of past goals (were they met; if not, why not?), and the employee and his or her supervisor then set new goals for the employee to achieve. These approaches (e.g., management by objectives[12] and performance planning and review[13]) strive to measure employee performance in a less subjective way by establishing goals that are easily quantified. Some examples of relatively objective goals are an increase of 5% in sales volume, a reduction of 10% in turnover, or an increase of 7% in productivity.

Table 3.5
BEHAVIORALLY BASED RATING SCALE

COMMUNICATING: Transmitting and receiving written and verbal information or instruction between the proper parties and following up to ensure that the message was received and understood.

High	7	Gives clear instructions and follows up to see that his or her people have what is needed to accomplish their job task.
	6	Passes along necessary verbal and written information based on the order of importance so that schedules will be met.
	5	Takes information as received and informs all departments that may be affected by that information.
Moderate	4	Receives instructions or information and reports back on job progress.
	3	Uses information sent to him or her, but does not relay information to other areas.
	2	Agrees to a job task without understanding what is involved and then does nothing to get the information or assistance needed to accomplish the task.
Low	1	Fails to pass information on to employees under his or her jurisdiction.

Because such goals can be measured with precision, there is little chance of misinterpretation of the standard on which the performance appraisal interview is based. Sales volume either increased 5% or it did not. A potential problem, however, is that the goals may not fairly reflect the individual employee's performance. Results are frequently influenced by many factors outside the control of the employee, such as economic conditions, regional variation in sales potential, and performance of other employees.

Another potential shortcoming of appraisal methods based on results arises in the nature of the feedback they provide to employees. As a supervisor, you give employees feedback to help them improve job performance in the future. Feedback about what goals have been achieved, however, may say little to employees about what they must do on a day-to-day basis to improve and achieve better results. Results are ends; performance is the means to those ends. For example, if you tell an employee that the sales quota was missed by 5%, this information alone is not very useful. The employee needs additional feedback about what was done on a day-to-day basis that contributed to the failure to accomplish the goal. For example, you and the employee need to discuss how well product knowledge was communicated, how well relationships with customers were established and maintained, how well a sale was closed, and so forth. To be useful, feedback should focus not only on what is achieved but also on the performance that contributed to the results. Therefore, performance appraisal interviews should contain feedback from appraisal methods from *both* columns II and III in Table 3.3 to be most useful to employees.

MAKING FEEDBACK USEFUL

Managers give employees feedback to help them develop themselves and maintain or improve their job performance. Another serious weakness in performance appraisal interviews is that often the feedback employees receive isn't useful to them; that is, it doesn't give them enough specific information and guidance to help them change their performance and results. The usefulness of the feedback is directly related to the method used to appraise performance. Useful feedback has four basic characteristics. Let's consider each of these in turn.

1. *Behavioral, not personal.* As we have already discussed, feedback should be given about what employees do or achieve, not about what they are or have. There are two basic reasons for this. First, personal feedback makes employees defensive. If

you are filling out trait-rating scales and are consequently passing judgment on your employees' basic character, you may threaten those employees' self-esteem. If you tell an employee that he or she does not have the right personality for sales, that employee is very likely to argue with you and claim that he or she has always been well liked and has gotten along well with people. If you rate an employee poor in attitude, that employee is likely to be insulted.

A second shortcoming of personal feedback is that it is not useful. Employees can seldom make use of assessments of their personal traits. Indeed, an employee may have the wrong personality for sales, but that employee has little control over his or her personality. People spend years in psychotherapy to change their personalities, and yet you're asking an employee to change his or her personality by this time next year! If, on the other hand, you tell the employee what he or she does on the job that leads you to conclude that his or her personality is poor or attitude is bad, the employee will find this feedback more useful. Employees have more control over how they behave. If you say

> "Every time we call a meeting, you arrive at least 15 minutes late."

> "When you arrive, you pull out a stack of files and begin paging through your paperwork."

> "Whenever someone makes a suggestion, you interrupt and say that the idea is worthless,"

the employee can use this feedback; the employee may not like what you have said, but he or she can alter arrival times, working on files, and interruptions. These behaviors can be controlled, and the employee has the potential to change them.

2. *Specific, not general.* Feedback in performance appraisal interviews is often given in general terms. If you tell employees that their work is good but could be better, if you encourage them to keep up the good work, or if you instruct them to be more cooperative with other departments, you will probably not

be very successful at changing their performance. This is not because your assessments are incorrect, but this kind of feedback is too general to give employees enough detailed information about what they have done that they need to change.

Instead, you need to give your employees feedback that specifies the behaviors they need to alter on a daily or weekly basis and the behaviors they should continue to maintain at a high level. Try to make your feedback specific and behavioral; you will find that it really affects how your employees perform in the future.

One of the cruel realities of performance appraisal is that praise is often given in general terms, but criticism is almost always specific. For example, an employee may be told:

> "We're very pleased with your performance in the technical area. This is a strength that's stood out in your work ever since you joined the company."

This general praise may encompass over 50% of the employee's job responsibilities, but it says very little about the specific functions that he or she is performing well. Consider the negative feedback:

> "...and you simply must communicate more effectively with the drafting department. Remember when you failed to tell them about the design changes on the Jackson project? Do you know how many extra hours we had to bill the client? 72! That put us 18% over budget. We just can't tolerate that kind of mistake."

This brings us to another characteristic of feedback.

3. *Balanced.* Because praise is typically general and criticism specific, time spent on criticism is often much greater than the time spent on praise. Many performance appraisal interviews are characterized by a "sandwich" approach. They begin with a minute or two of general praise, followed by that telltale word "but" or "however." Then comes 25 minutes of discussion about the problem areas and ways in which the employee needs to improve. The interview then ends with a brief dose of reassuring praise. The

result is an interview in which the majority of time was spent on what the employee has done wrong. And yet that same employee may be performing acceptably well on the majority of the responsibilities that make up the job.

It is important for you to maintain a balance between positive and negative feedback in the interview. Time spent on each should roughly match the proportion of acceptable and unacceptable job performance of the employee being appraised. Unfortunately, many supervisors ignore positive performance and focus only on negative feedback in their interactions with employees. This practice reflects the philosophy that "no news is good news" and creates a climate in which employees are seldom praised and assume that they have done something wrong whenever the boss calls them into his or her office. You can achieve a better balance in your performance appraisal interviews by following the first two guidelines. Give specific, behavioral feedback about not only the job areas in which employees need to improve, but also the areas in which they are performing well.

4. *Future oriented.* The past is dead and should not be belabored in a performance appraisal interview. Rather, it should serve as a springboard for planning for the future. After a thorough discussion of an employee's performance, it is important that you turn your attention to the future and set some goals before you complete the interview. And, remember, these goals are most likely to be achieved if they are specific. General goals such as "being more cooperative" or "trying harder" are less likely to lead to improved performance. Like New Year's resolutions, they are easily set and just as easily forgotten. Furthermore, general goals provide unclear targets. Employees may be highly motivated to change, but general goals like "improving my attitude" or "working harder to meet the sales quota" are too vague to specify where employees should direct their energy and what aspects of their performance they should change.

Finally, whenever possible, goals should also be mutually endorsed by both you and your employee. People are more highly committed to goals they set for themselves than to those they are instructed to achieve. Therefore, a performance appraisal interview in which employees set their own specific goals is most likely to lead to changes in performance. Later in this chapter I will discuss how you can encourage employees to set their own performance goals.

PLANNING SUCCESSFUL PERFORMANCE APPRAISAL INTERVIEWS

So far, I have stressed what you need to do *before* the interview to make it successful. Separating the performance appraisal interview, which deals with employee development and performance improvement, from the salary review interview, which focuses on communicating and supporting administrative decisions, is a good beginning. In addition, in each interview you conduct, you need to concentrate on the objectives of the performance appraisal interview that are pertinent to that employee's interests and goals. Finally, the method used by your organization to appraise employee performance is crucial because it determines the nature of the feedback you give your employees during the interview. If you make the feedback useful to your employees and they see it as fair and truly representative of what they have actually done on the job, your interviews are much more likely to be successful.

CONDUCTING THE PERFORMANCE APPRAISAL INTERVIEW

Approach

Regardless of how well you have planned the interview, it will fail if you do not conduct it properly. Discovering an approach to conducting the interview that works for them often looms as a serious struggle for supervisors and managers. Proceeding as you usually do in your daily contact with employees is not likely to work. The performance appraisal interview is *different*. It is more formal and more important than the typical interactions you have with your employees.

How can you approach this troublesome interview? Norman Maier[14] identified three fundamental approaches to conducting performance appraisal interviews. Just as I have done, Maier limited the appraisal interview to those objectives that involve employee development and performance improvement. Consequently, his three basic approaches do not address administrative matters like salary increases or promotions.

Maier named the three approaches "tell and sell," "tell and listen," and "problem solving." The basic ingredients of each approach are outlined in Table 3.6. As you read through the following summaries, you may recognize yourself or your supervisor.

Tell and sell. Here the supervisor's main intention is to tell employees what is right and wrong with their performance and what changes are necessary in the future. The supervisor then strives to convince the employee to accept this judgment. The supervisor assumes the role of all-powerful and all-knowing judge of the employee and uses various persuasive and pressure techniques to get the employee to accept the judgment. Since many employees object to being told off like children and raise counter-arguments to the supervisor's views, this approach can degenerate into a shouting match.

Tell and listen. In this approach the supervisor also serves as a judge of employees and tells them what is right and wrong with their past performance. This approach is based on the assumption that the boss has all the answers, and, to get employees to improve their performance, he or she must merely communicate those answers to the employees. After the telling is done, however, the supervisor does not press the employee to accept this judgment, as was done in "tell and sell." Instead, the supervisor becomes very non-directive and lets the employees vent their feelings of disappointment and defensiveness. The supervisor allows the employees to complain

Table 3.6

THREE TYPES OF PERFORMANCE APPRAISAL INTERVIEWS

Method (Role of Interviewer)	Tell and sell (Judge)	Tell and listen (Judge)	Problem solving (Helper)
Objectives	To communicate evaluation. To persuade employee to improve	To communicate evaluation. To release defensive feelings	To stimulate growth and development in employee
Assumptions	A supervisor is qualified to evaluate an employee. Employees can correct faults if they want to	People will change if defensive feelings are released	Growth can occur without correcting faults
Reactions	Defensiveness. Attempts to cover anger	Anger is expressed. Employee feels accepted	Problem solving
Skills	Salesmanship. Patience	Listening and reflecting feelings. Summarizing	Listening and reflecting feelings and ideas. Asking probing questions. Summarizing
Attitude	People profit from criticism and appreciate help	People can respect the feelings of others	Discussion develops new ideas and mutual interests
Gains	Success most likely when employee respects boss	Employee sees that the boss is caring	Almost assured of some improvements
Risks	Loss of loyalty. Face-saving problems created	Need for change may not be developed. Discourages independence	Employee may lack ideas. Proposals may not be what the boss had in mind

about how they were evaluated and remains very understanding and sympathetic during this period in the interview. The assumption is that, if employees are allowed to express their feelings of disappointment and resentment, they will be more likely to accept the supervisor's judgment ultimately. Note that there is more upward communication in this interview than in "tell and sell," but the employees still contribute nothing to the supervisor's evaluation of their performance. The supervisor is still the all-knowing and all-powerful judge.

Problem solving. In the problem-solving approach, the role of the supervisor shifts from judge to helper. The supervisor's intention is to allow employees to evaluate their own performance, identify their own areas of needed improvement, and set their own developmental and work goals. The supervisor begins the interview by asking employees to evaluate their own performance. During this discussion the supervisor uses nondirective skills such as paraphrasing ideas and reflecting feelings, asking for elaboration and clarification, and summarizing to draw out the employee's ideas and evaluation. There is a strong orientation toward the future in this interview, as employees are encouraged to set goals for improved performance and to identify steps necessary to meet these goals. These steps may include informal assistance from the supervisor or more formal training courses, or even changes in job responsibilities.

The Risks

As Maier points out, each of these three approaches may be appropriate for a specific employee. Young, inexperienced employees who respect their supervisor's judgment may respond well to a tell-and-sell interview. For experienced employees with good awareness of their own performance and sensible ideas for improvement, a problem-solving approach may work best.

Unfortunately, however, each of these three approaches may also fail. The problem-solving approach has its pitfalls. When asked for a self-appraisal, the employee may say very little or may fail to raise the problems the supervisor wishes to address. When asked for goals, the employee may have none to offer. Another risk of the problem-solving interview is that the employee may have plenty to say, but it may not be what the supervisor wants to hear. The employee may evaluate his or her performance quite differently than the supervisor has evaluated the employee. The employee may also propose goals that the supervisor feels are inappropriate.

The tell-and-sell and tell-and-listen approaches run a particularly high risk of failure. The supervisor may be wrong in his or her appraisal of the employee's performance. Furthermore, the supervisor may be incorrect in assessing the *causes* of the employee's performance and may make inappropriate suggestions for improvement. For example, a supervisor might send a highly skilled employee on a training course rather than probing to learn *from the employee* that he or she is bored with a specific job responsibility. The appropriate corrective action is either to change the nature of the job or find a way to increase the employee's level of motivation. In addition, being told what they are doing wrong and how they must change can make employees defensive and angry. Finally, the telling interviews reduce communication from the employee to the supervisor to a minimum and can thoroughly demoralize employees who have good understanding of their own performance and positive proposals to contribute to the interview.

The Burke-Stanley case, summarized here and expanded in detail at the end of this chapter, illustrates the devastating effects of the tell-and-sell approach. In this case George Stanley, the head of the electrical section in the Engineering Department of a construction company, has mixed feelings about the performance of Tom Burke, one of his eight supervisors. Since being promoted two years ago, Burke has grown to be the most technically creative and productive supervisor reporting to Stanley. But Burke has achieved his high productivity by concentrating on his own group and reducing his level of cooperation with his fellow supervisors, and by turning down routine projects so his staff can work on the most challenging work in the section. Furthermore, employee turnover is higher among Burke's staff than in any other unit in Stanley's section.

> STANLEY: "In our interview today I'd like to outline your performance as I see it, and I'd appreciate your comments. I feel that in the technical area you've been most strong, both in creativity and originality. This has been typical of you throughout your years of employment even before you became a supervisor. The productivity in your department is very high, and I feel that you are quite effective in utilizing your staff."

This is a typical beginning of a "telling" interview in which the boss begins with brief, general praise and then turns to a more detailed discussion of specific problems in the employee's performance.

> BURKE: "We've got a good bunch."

> STANLEY: "Good bunch, have you? I think we need to spend some time on some areas of your performance that we have talked about before. I feel we should discuss them in more detail now. It seems that recently you're having some problems cooperating with your fellow supervisors. There is some indication that you are not sharing your expertise with them. What do you see as the problem in that area?"

Notice that Stanley ignores Burke's comment about his staff and turns from general praise to a negative point, which he labels as a problem.

> BURKE: "Well, I used to help them out, but the more we did for them, the more they expected. They'll never raise their efficiency the way we have in our department. I guess they're doing the best they can, but you really can't single out one department; efficiency is a plant-wide thing."

> STANLEY: "But don't you think that with all the expertise and knowledge you have that you can benefit the company by helping out the other supervisors?"

> BURKE: "But I have tried to help them. If you're assessing the potential of my employees, my young junior designer, Andrea Dobbs, could probably do about any supervisory job in the place. Now there's spreading our expertise into another department if she were made a supervisor."

> STANLEY: "I'm more concerned, though, Tom, with the apparent lack of cooperation between you and the other supervisors in the department and the interaction which appears to be missing. Do you not feel that working closer with these other people would only help to improve the overall situation?"

Burke and Stanley have gotten into a "Yea, but" pattern of conversation, in which each is on the defensive and simply continues to state his own argument rather than really listening to the other's point of view and confronting the issue directly. Notice that Stanley ignores Burke's proposal to promote Dobbs and presses on with his point.

> BURKE: "Well, if you remember, I did work pretty closely with them for over a year, and I slowly had to stop it. I can spread myself only so thin. I didn't see any improvement in the other supervisors' productivity. And I do have my own department to look after."

Again, Stanley fails to respond to what Burke says.

> STANLEY: "Well, this is a problem that we're going to have to solve in one way or another, Tom. We may have to help you out with your work load, but I do feel that the contribution you can make to the company as a whole is lacking at this point. We're going to have to work very strongly on this."

> BURKE: "You're the boss."

STANLEY: "Another thing that's become apparent recently has been seemingly low morale among your employees. I have noticed an increase in your turnover figures, and replacing your employees has cost us far too much in the past quarter."

The interview continues in this vein. Stanley raises additional problems about Burke's attitude, his desire to have the most interesting projects in the section assigned to his group, and his view that he is more productive than the other supervisors. Burke continues to argue or give lip service to Stanley's proposals, but there is little likelihood that Burke will perform differently next year.

Some important issues in the case must be addressed. Burke must take his share of the routine projects of the section, and all eight supervisors need to consult and work with one another more closely. Some changes are also necessary to reduce turnover in the entire company. How these issues are addressed, however, is critical. With an experienced employee like Tom Burke, the tell-and-sell approach is very unlikely to be effective.

An Alternative: Two-way Communication

What we need is an approach to the performance appraisal interview that combines the strengths of Maier's three methods but minimizes the risks of each. My recommendation is a composite of the problem-solving and telling types of interviews. It is quite clear that beginning with a telling approach will make it almost impossible to shift in the same interview to a problem-solving approach. Once the supervisor has snuffed out an employee's attempts to be heard, it is unlikely that the employee will open up later in the interview. Therefore, a more effective interview begins with problem solving and then shifts to a tell if necessary.

An obvious key to two-way communication is to encourage employees to talk about their own performance. Most employees are aware of what they do well at work (positive feedback), and

Table 3.7
FEEDBACK GUIDE

	Positive Feedback	Areas for Improvement
Employee Aware	I	III
Employee Unaware	II	IV

what they want to or need to do better (areas for improvement). But there are sometimes things that they do well, or they can improve, that employees are not aware of. These aspects of employee performance are shown in Table 3.7

The secret to constructive, two-way communication in the performance appraisal interview is to encourage employees to raise not only what they do well on the job (Cell I), but also those areas in which they want to or need to improve (Cell III). Supervisors and managers can increase employees' awareness of both positive performance and areas for improvement (and thus reduce the size of Cells II and IV) by providing employees regularly with specific, behavioral, balanced feedback, as discussed earlier in this chapter. If this is done, there should be no surprises during the performance appraisal interview. To ensure two-way communication in the appraisal interview, I recommend that you prepare for the interview carefully and cover all your objectives by following the format in Table 3.8.

Before the Interview

As a supervisor or manager, you must do your homework before the interview. Begin with an informal or formal appraisal of the performance of each of your employees. Consider the employee's performance and results, and your ideas for employee

Table 3.8
PLANNING THE PERFORMANCE
APPRAISAL INTERVIEW

I. **Before the Interview**

    A. Carefully evaluate the employee's performance and results

    B. Set a meeting and clearly state its purpose

    C. Ask the employee to:
        1. Do a self appraisal
        2. Set work and developmental goals

II. **Format**

    A. Restate the purpose of the interview

    B. Encourage the employee to talk about past performance and results

    C. Focus on positive topics (I) and probe; Raise additional positive topics (II), if necessary, and probe

    D. Focus on areas for improvement (III) and probe

    E. Raise additional areas for improvement (IV), if necessary, and probe

    F. Set mutual, specific goals

    G. Propose follow-up to ensure change

---

development. If your organization uses an appraisal form, refer to it to help you structure your thinking. You will enter the interview with an agenda containing your assessments of the employee's past performance (positive feedback and areas for improvement) and your ideas of how he or she can improve.

To maximize upward communication in the interview, you must encourage the employee to do some homework, too. Schedule the meeting about a week ahead of time and explain its purpose to your employee. In addition, ask your employee to think about two topics: (1) how well he or she has performed since the last appraisal interview and (2) his or her work goals and developmental plans in the forthcoming year. What form the employee's preparation takes depends on the nature of the organization's performance appraisal system. In a results-oriented system like management by objectives, employees will review past goals and set new goals for the future. In a system where performance is evaluated formally, employees may rate their own performance on a checklist or rating scale. Whatever the approach to performance appraisal, it is important that employees enter the interview having looked both to the past and to the future.

Format

As mentioned earlier, a key to success in the performance appraisal interview is to follow a format that ensures two-way communication. A good plan is to begin with *upward communication* by drawing out the employee's views of his or her performance, results, and plans for improvement. You can add your own views as the discussion proceeds. But don't begin the interview by presenting your evaluation of the employee's performance, because that is a telling approach.

Restate the purpose of the interview. As you did when you scheduled the meeting, clearly state the objectives of this interview. Simply saying that the time has come for you to meet with each of your employees to discuss how they have performed during the past year (or six months or quarter) and to hear their plans for the next year is a clear way to begin.

Encourage the employee to talk about past performance and results. As a supervisor or manager, you have the responsibility of evaluating your employees' performance as well as helping them to improve. You will enter the interview with an agenda. You will have already completed an evaluation of the employee's performance, identifying areas of work where the employee is effective and areas in which you feel improvement is needed. In addition, you will have formed hunches about the *causes* of employee performance and ideas for employee development. Your goals in this early stage of the interview are (1) to encourage the employee to raise some of your agenda items and (2) to learn as much as possible about how, why, and how well the employee has performed each job responsibility and what plans the employee has for improvement. To achieve these goals you need to begin an *information-collecting sequence* for conducting the performance appraisal interview: initiate, listen, focus, probe, plan (Table 3.9).

Initiate the discussion with an open-ended question such as:

"How would you rate your performance over this past year?"

or

"What do you think of your performance over the past year?"

or

"What goals do you feel you have achieved during this past year?"

As the employee responds you need to listen very carefully, not only for aspects of performance the employee is pleased with (Cell I in Table 3.7) but also areas for improvement (Cell III).

Some supervisors have told me that their employees will not assess their own performance when asked these questions. But the same supervisors have been surprised by the amount of talking their employees have done when they actually tried these techniques in performance appraisal interviews. In my experience, nearly all employees have a lot to say about their own performance and plans for improvements, *when they are asked.*

Focus on positive topics and probe each. Here is where the tone of the interview is set. In response to the open-ended question, most employees will raise positive topics (Cell I) and many will also raise some concerns or dissatisfactions (Cell III). I suggest that you begin with the positives the employee raises and *probe them in detail* as shown in Table 3.9. You must resist the temptation to jump to the "telling" portion of the interview or to focus only on your agenda items. Be patient and dig for what the employee

Table 3.9
INFORMATION-COLLECTING SEQUENCE

	Step	Example
1.	INITIATE—Use open-ended questions to get the employee talking about how he or she has performed.	"How would you rate your performance this past year?" "What goals did you work toward this past year?" "How do you feel about your performance this past year?"
2.	LISTEN—Listen for topics to be probed.	Listen for your employee's achievements as well as awareness of areas of needed improvement.
3.	FOCUS—Direct employee's attention first to positive topics and later to areas of needed improvement.	"You mentioned..." "I'm particularly interested in..."
	If the employee raises no areas of needed improvement, ask for them.	"We've had a chance to discuss some of your achievements. Any areas where you think you can improve?" or "Any frustrations or concerns?"
4.	PROBE—Delve into topics you focused on to learn more details.	HOW—"What approach; what was involved?" WHY—"Why did you use that approach?" RESULTS—"How well; what results?"
5.	PLAN—Encourage the employee to consider changes.	"What would you do differently next time?" "How can you increase your potential to perform this part of your job?"

If employees set work or developmental goals that you endorse but cannot implement, explain the constraints directly and honestly.

has to contribute. If, for example, an employee's answer to the open-ended question is, "I think I've done fine," the ball is very abruptly back in your court. You can come back with a more specific question to keep the employee talking. For example, "Well, I'm pleased to hear that you feel that way. What are some of the things you've done that you are particularly pleased with?"

As the employee raises topics, store them in your memory to bring up at the appropriate time for further discussion. Let's consider, for example, the case of Tom Burke and George Stanley. Suppose Burke raises the technical performance of his group and his concern about his relationship with the other supervisors. Avoid the trap of jumping on Tom's problems with the other supervisors as soon as it is raised. Focus first on the positive and begin the probing sequence with a "how" question, as in the following illustration.

> STANLEY: "You mentioned that your group has been particularly productive technically, Tom. What steps have you taken to help the group reach this level of productivity?"

> BURKE: "I know my employees' strengths and weaknesses, and I assign each of them work that they do best."

> STANLEY: "So you specialize your people." (paraphrase) Why do you make work assignments that way, Tom?"

> BURKE: "Well, George, you know how much pressure we've had for productivity in the last 18 months. I figured it was the best way to get maximum efficiency from my department."

> STANLEY: "Yes, top management has had us all under a lot of pressure lately. How has this approach worked out for you, Tom?" (*How well* probe)

> BURKE: "Very well, George. Our productivity is the best in the company."

> STANLEY: "Now that you've worked with this approach for a while, Tom, would you do anything differently in the future?" (Stanley asks for Tom's plans for improvement.)

> BURKE: "I've got to admit that there's a down side, too. I've had several people leave the company for better opportunities outside. I'm afraid some of them feel too specialized. And you know how difficult it is to get someone promoted here, George." (Through this probing, Stanley gets Burke to evaluate his own method and raise the issue of turnover in his department.)

> STANLEY: "As you know, Tom, turnover is a fact of life in this business, but your turnover rate is pretty high. Any ideas of how we can bring it down?"

As the discussion continues, Burke and Stanley consider the options of cross training and job rotation in Burke's department, along with transfering some of Burke's employees into other departments in the section.

After you have focused on and probed into all the positive topics your employee raises, then move into Cell II in Table 3.7 and raise additional positive topics that have not been discussed yet and probe them in detail. Detailed probing into the positive topics is important for two reasons. First, it allows you to learn not only *what* your employees think they do well, but also their work methods, their rationale, and the results of their efforts. The "why" question is particularly important because it uncovers the *causes* of employee performance. Second, the "plan" probe gives employees a chance to propose their own ideas for improvement. Furthermore, when you probe the positive aspects of employee performance in depth and ask employees what they would do differently, they frequently make suggestions on how to improve their performance. They are more likely to be committed to their own proposals than to changes you tell them to make.

Focus on areas for improvement and probe each. After you have discussed topics in Cells I and II of Table 3.7, turn to any areas for improvement mentioned by the employee (Cell III). When you address areas for improvement, you are likely to encounter strong feelings. *A rule of thumb is to deal with the feelings first.* Tom alluded to his relationship with the other supervisors in response to George's open-ended question. Turning to Cell III, George can bring it up again in the following way:

STANLEY: "I gather from what you said earlier, Tom, that you're concerned with your working relationship with the other supervisors."

BURKE: "Yea, they're acting like a bunch of jerks. They will hardly talk to me anymore!"

STANLEY: "You don't sound very happy about that." (Stanley reflects Burke's feeling.)

BURKE: "Well, I'm not. It really bugs me when the deadwood around here just leans on me."

STANLEY: "Pretty frustrating situation, that's for sure."

BURKE: "I think we should fire the whole bunch of them!"

STANLEY: "It seems as though you're about at the end of your rope."

BURKE: "Well, I am. I just don't know what else can be done. I'm under tremendous pressure to maintain my department's productivity, and yet the other supervisors want me to help them out, too."

STANLEY: "So you feel in conflict, Tom. Either you keep up your productivity or you help out in other departments. (Stanley gets to the core of the problem and then begins probing.) Let's start at the beginning. Give me your view of what has happened between you and the other supervisors in the last year. Let's begin with when and how you began cutting back on the amount of help you gave them."

Notice that Stanley shows awareness of the pain and frustration that Burke is experiencing and gives him an opportunity to vent those feelings before probing to get a rational, less emotional explanation from Burke. Burke has said, in exasperation, some things he probably doesn't really mean. It is crucial that Stanley not lecture or scold Burke about his feelings. For example, after their first exchange, Stanley would make a mistake if he embarked on a lecture about how communication and cooperation are essential. Similarly, when Burke refers to his colleagues as "deadwood" and proposes that they be fired, Stanley must avoid scolding Burke for making such comments about them. Doing so at this time would only push Burke into a corner and force him to defend statements he probably doesn't fully endorse.

In dealing with Burke's feelings, Stanley is able to get to the cause of Tom's frustration; namely, the conflict between maintaining his productivity and assisting other supervisors. As Stanley probes further, he discovers that Burke cut down his interaction with other supervisors about a year ago quite abruptly and with no discussion (how) because he felt under tremendous pressure and didn't know what else to do (why). When asked how this method has worked out for him, Burke assesses it as disastrous. Finally, when asked what he would do differently, Burke explains that he would have talked it over first with Stanley and then in a meeting with the other supervisors. From that discussion, Burke and Stanley agree to hold a section meeting to address this issue and make plans for improving communication and collaboration among all department supervisors. Emphasis in this part of the interview is on collecting information from the employee. The interviewer should do as little telling as possible.

I want to be clear here. Supervisors should not necessarily avoid confrontations in the performance appraisal interview. For example, if Burke still endorses a strong negative view of his colleagues and sticks to his proposal that they all be fired even after he has vented his emotions, Stanley must state clearly that he does not agree. But the timing is crucial. Disagreements early in the interview will likely succeed only in reducing communication. This point is illustrated well in the contrast between the excerpt from the tell-and-sell interview presented earlier in this chapter and the example just discussed. In the short tell-and-tell excerpt, Stanley completely ignores Burke's feelings and proposals and essentially lectures Burke, but this approach leads to no clear solution. In the example just discussed, however, Stanley responds to the feelings, and they work together to develop a specific idea to remedy the problem.

Raise additional areas for improvement, if necessary. To this point the performance appraisal interview has the character of Maier's problem-solving approach. This phase of the interview may last only a few minutes with some employees and perhaps an hour with others. By beginning this way, you are allowing for as much upward communication as possible. There are some risks to this approach, however. Employees may have little to say about their performance, or their own evaluations may differ significantly from the supervisor's appraisal. Finally, they may not raise all the topics on your agenda.

The next stage of the interview, therefore, is designed for you to do some telling, if necessary. Suppose the employee has raised many positive topics, but has said nothing about areas for improvement (Cell III in Table 3.7). After you have focused on the positives raised by the employee (Cell I) or by yourself (Cell II) and probed them in detail, you can ask the employee to raise some areas for improvement by saying, "We've had a chance to discuss some of your achievements. Any areas where you think you can improve?" If the employee still raises none, and you have rated the employee low in some areas of performance, you then move into Cell IV and raise them yourself. It is important to note that this telling follows a period of discussion of the employee's topics. Consequently, the employee is now likely to be receptive to your views. If you have done ratings or some other form of written evaluation, this is the time to show them to the employee. I want to stress that, as soon as you place an evaluation form on the desk and refer to it, the interview becomes a "telling" interview. Once the telling phase begins, it is almost impossible to change to the problem-solving approach with its emphasis on upward communication. Therefore, I advise you to avoid the temptation of beginning the interview with a discussion of your ratings of employee performance. In fact, you may learn something from the employee in the early stages of the interview that influences you to revise your ratings.

Set mutual, specific goals. On the basis of the discussion to this point, you and your employee should have already identified some plans for improvement. Before closing the interview, it is useful to summarize the goals and ensure that they are as specific as possible and are ideally endorsed by both parties.

Propose follow-up. Plans for change, like New Year's resolutions, may be made in the fervor of the moment and quickly forgotten. It is very useful to conclude the interview by deciding explicitly who will do what, by when, to ensure that the work goals and developmental plans proposed by you and your employee are carried out. This step will also enable you and the employee to monitor his or her progress on the goals.

Team Approach to Performance Appraisal

So far, this chapter has focused on the most common approach to performance appraisal, in which the immediate supervisor evaluates an employee's performance and conducts the appraisal interview. In a growing number of organizations, however, employees evaluate the performance of their peers and even their supervisors.[16] In particular, employers that practice participative management or operate with self-managed work teams have adopted a partnership approach to performance appraisal in which each team member evaluates his or her own performance as well as the performance of all other team members, including the team leader.

The "telling" approaches to performance appraisal interviews are inappropriate for team performance appraisal because the evaluator does not have formal authority over the employee being evaluated. Instead, a two-way discussion between equals is needed. This chapter's approach to two-way communication in the interview, outlined in Tables 3.8 and 3.9, can be used very effectively in team performance appraisal.

INTERVIEW STYLE, SUPERVISORY STYLE, AND ORGANIZATIONAL CULTURE

As with all interviews covered in this book, the approach I recommend includes a good degree of flexibility, and you must tailor it to your own personal style and organization. You must conduct the performance appraisal interview in a way that is consistent with your style of supervision. For example, the autocrat who tries to foster two-way communication will be viewed with suspicion and even disbelief by employees. Such a boss may be better off with a tell-and-sell approach. If you practice a consultative or participative style of management, however, you will find my approach to the interview quite compatible.

How successfully you implement the principles of this chapter will also be strongly influenced by your organization's work culture and the recent history of performance appraisal in your organization. Many of today's employers have moved away from the autocratic style of management and have tried to create a culture of teamwork and cooperation between supervisors and employees. And, yet, the performance appraisal forms, policies and practices of these same employers continue to place the supervisor in the role of a judge. This inconsistency leads to many of the problems with performance appraisal discussed in this chapter.

Most organizations need to revise their methods of appraising performance; most evaluate people, not performance. Many appraisal systems put far too much emphasis on grading or scoring employees, rather than developing them. Moreover, many supervisors and managers conduct "telling" interviews because they perceive their role as judge. Employees learn to mistrust this kind of performance appraisal system, and overcoming that negative culture will take time. Separating annual salary review discussions from performance appraisal interviews, which you conduct as often as necessary to help develop employees and improve their performance, is an important first step. Discussing performance with your employees in specific, behavioral, balanced terms will also help make employees more receptive to performance appraisal.

One expert[17] on performance appraisal recently made the rather unorthodox recommendation that ratings of employee performance be dropped entirely from appraisal systems, so the discussion can focus solely on developing employees and improving their performance. In fact, I have helped several organizations carry out this recommendation.

For instance, some groups of supervisors and managers had identified and defined the critical dimensions of performance they wanted to include in the performance appraisal form and then discuss with their employees during developmental sessions. But the newly created form contained no numbers for rating employee performance. When supervisors and employees met periodically to discuss ways to develop employees and improve their performance, the appraisal form was used to focus the discussion on crucial areas of performance, but not to rate or score employees. As the supervisors proceeded through the probes discussed earlier in this chapter (how, why, results, do differently?), many employees assessed their own performance and set developmental and work goals. These organizations have reported a marked improvement in employee morale because performance appraisal interviews have become a form of positive communication. Supervisors and employees now discuss employee performance openly and generate excellent ideas for improving the performance of the employees and the entire department.

INTERVIEW TRANSCRIPT

This section contains a transcript of a performance appraisal interview conducted with an emphasis on two-way communication. The interview is based on the following case[18] involving George Stanley, a section head in the engineering department of a construction company, and Tom Burke, a supervisor who reports to Stanley. The transcript is based on an actual interview conducted with the Burke-Stanley role-playing case in a training course. As a role play, it is not as detailed or complex as performance appraisal interviews you might conduct with actual employees, but it clearly illustrates how strongly the interviewer's approach can influence the response of the employee and the outcome of the discussion.

General Instructions

George Stanley is the electrical section head in the Engineering Department of the Quality Construction Company. The work in the department includes design, drafting, cost estimates, keeping maps up to date, checking standards and building codes, field inspection and follow-up, and so on. Eight first-line supervisors report to Stanley. The duties of the supervisors are partly technical and partly supervisory. The organizational chart for Stanley's section is shown below.

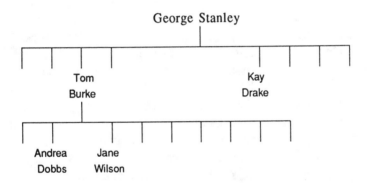

Company policy requires that all section heads interview each of their supervisors once a year, the purpose being:

1. To evaluate the supervisor's performance during the year,

2. To give recognition for jobs well done, and

3. To correct weaknesses.

The company believes that employees should know how they stand and that everything should be done to develop management personnel. The evaluation interviews were introduced to serve this purpose.

Tom Burke is one of the supervisors reporting to Stanley. He has a college degree in electrical engineering and in addition to his technical duties, which often take him to the field, he supervises the work of one junior designer, six drafters, and two clerks. He is highly paid as are all the supervisors in this department because of the high requirements in technical knowledge. Burke has been with the company for 12 years and has been a supervisor for two years. He is married and has two children. He owns his home and is active in civic affairs in his community.

Role for Tom Burke, First-line Supervisor in the Engineering Department

One junior designer, six drafters, and two clerks report to you. You feel that you get along fine with your employees. You have always been pretty much of an idea man and apparently have the knack of passing on your enthusiasm to others. There is a lot of "we" feeling in your unit because it is obvious that your group is the most productive in the section.

You believe in developing your employees and try to give them tough assignments. You view each employee as a specialist and assign work he or she does best. This helps you keep your group's productivity up. You have gained a reputation for developing your people because they frequently go elsewhere and get better jobs. Since promotion is slow in the company, turnover in your unit is higher than in others, but you were pleased that one of your clerks, Jane Wilson, turned down an outside offer for a 10% salary increase because she likes working for you. You want to get her a raise as soon as possible.

The other supervisors in George Stanley's section do not have your enthusiasm. Some are pretty dull and unimaginative. During your first year as supervisor you used to help them a lot, but you soon found that they leaned on you and before long you were doing their work. There's a lot of pressure for production and since you got your promotion by producing, you don't intend to let other supervisors interfere. So you've cut back on helping them, and your production has increased, but a couple of them are pretty sore at you.

Stanley should realize that some of the supervisors are weak and assign more routine jobs to their units. Then they wouldn't need your help and you could concentrate on jobs that suit your unit. At present, Stanley passes out work pretty much as he gets it. Since you are efficient, you get more than your share of the section's jobs, and you don't see why the extra jobs couldn't be more interesting. This would motivate units to turn out more work. When you suggested to Stanley that he turn over some of the more routine jobs to other units he did it, but he sure was reluctant.

You did one thing recently that bothered you. There was a design change in a set of plans and you should have told Kay Drake (a fellow supervisor) about it, but it slipped your mind. Kay was out when you thought about it and then you got involved in a hot idea with Andrea Dobbs, your Junior Designer, and forgot to get back to Drake. As a result, she had to do a lot of extra work and blamed you for the trouble. You apologized and offered to help, but she turned down your offer.

Today you have an interview with George Stanley. It's about this employee development plan for the company. It shouldn't take very long, but it's nice to have the boss tell you about the good work you're turning out. Maybe there's a raise in it; maybe he'll tell you something about what to expect in the future.

Role for George Stanley, Section Head of the Engineering Department

You have evaluated all the supervisors reporting to you, and during the next two weeks will interview each of them. You hope to use these interviews constructively to develop each employee. Today you have arranged to interview Tom Burke, one of your eight first-line supervisors. Tom has been with the company 12 years, the last two years as a supervisor. He has a college degree, is married, and has two children.

Tom is highly creative, original, and exceptionally competent technically. His unit is very productive and has made steady improvement during the two years under his supervision. Within the past six months you have given him extra work and he has gotten it done on schedule. As far as productivity and dependability are concerned, he is your top supervisor.

His cooperation with other supervisors in the section, however, leaves much to be desired. Before you made him a supervisor, his originality and technical knowledge were available to your whole section. Gradually he has withdrawn and now acts more as a lone wolf. You've asked other supervisors to talk over certain technical problems with him, but they tell you he seldom offers suggestions. He tells them he's busy or listens as if he's not interested, kids them, or makes sarcastic remarks, depending on his mood. On one occasion he allowed another supervisor, Kay Drake, to make a mistake that could have been avoided if Burke had kept Kay informed about the status of certain design changes Burke knew about. You certainly expect supervisors to keep in touch about important matters like design changes that can affect the whole section.

Furthermore, during the past six months Tom has been unwilling to take two assignments. He said they were routine, that he preferred more interesting work, and he advised you to give them to other supervisors. To prevent trouble, you followed his suggestion, but you can't give him all the interesting work without affecting the morale of the other supervisors.

Burke's failure to cooperate has you worried for another reason. Although his group is highly productive, his turnover is higher than in other groups. You have heard no complaints yet, but you suspect he may be treating his employees in an arbitrary manner. Certainly if he is abrupt with the other supervisors, he's likely to be even more so with his people. You suspect the high productivity in his group is not due to high morale, but to his practice of using his staff to do work each one does best. This method won't develop his staff or continue to challenge them, and it may be contributing to the high turnover in Burke's unit.

You hope to discuss these matters with Burke in such a way as to recognize his good points and at the same time correct some of his weaknesses.

> STANLEY: "As I said last week when we set up this appointment, Tom, this is our annual performance review meeting. I'd like to get your views on your performance over the past year and discuss your plans for the upcoming year."
>
> BURKE: "Fine, that sounds good to me."
>
> STANLEY: "I'm glad to hear you feel that way, Tom. I'd like to begin by asking you how you would assess your performance over this past year."

After restating the purpose of the interview, Stanley begins with an open-ended question to invite Burke to volunteer his views.

> BURKE: "Well, George, I feel it's been a pretty good year, all things considered."
>
> STANLEY: "So you feel generally satisfied, then. Is there anything that stands out in your mind?"
>
> BURKE: "I'm particularly pleased with the group reporting to me. They're a really good bunch, we pull together real well, and our productivity is the highest in the company."
>
> STANLEY: "You sound really excited about your group, Tom. You mentioned that your employees have been particularly productive. What steps have you taken to help the group reach this level of productivity?"

Stanley focuses on a positive point and begins probing with a "how" question.

> BURKE: "I know my employees' strengths and weaknesses, and I assign each of them work that they do best."

STANLEY: "So you specialize your people. Why do you make work assignments that way, Tom?"

BURKE: "Well, George, you know how much pressure we've had for productivity in the last 18 months. I figured it was the best way to get maximum efficiency from my department."

STANLEY: "Yes, top management has had us all under a lot of pressure lately. How has this approach worked out for you?"

BURKE: "Very well, George. Our productivity is the best in the company."

STANLEY: "That's true, Tom, and we really appreciate the efforts of you and your people. Now that you've worked with this approach for a while, would you do anything differently in the future?"

BURKE: "I've got to admit that there's a down side, too. I've had several people leave the company for better opportunities outside. I'm afraid some of them feel too specialized. And you know how difficult it is to get someone promoted here, George."

Through this probing, Stanley gets Burke to evaluate his own method and raise the issue of turnover in his department. He now focuses on it carefully.

STANLEY: "As you know, Tom, turnover is a fact of life in this business, but your turnover rate is pretty high. Any ideas of how we can bring it down?"

BURKE: "I'm not sure, George, but we've got to do something about the lack of promotion in the section. I hate to lose such fine employees." I've got a junior designer, Andrea Dobbs, who's overdue for a promotion right now and I'm afraid she might quit."

STANLEY: "I share your frustration about the turnover, Tom, and I would certainly hate to lose Andrea. Maybe we can find a way to move them around inside the company or give them new assignments to keep them challenged and interested."

BURKE: "I've thought about that, George, but then I'd lose my specialists and my productivity would go down."

STANLEY: "I can see your dilemma, Tom." I think in the long run your group and the company would benefit if you sacrificed some productivity to reduce our turnover costs. What do you think of cross-training some of your staff, and even moving some people like Andrea into another department?"

BURKE: "Well, I guess it's better for me to lose them to someone else in our company than to one of our competitors."

STANLEY: "I agree, Tom. Can you consider each member of your group as a possible candidate for job rotation within your department or transfer to another department?"

BURKE: "I think that's a good plan, George, if you will tolerate a drop in productivity."

STANLEY: "Let's consider your ideas for changing your employees' work assignments and estimate the size of your drop in productivity. Can you have a detailed plan for me within four weeks?"

BURKE: "You'll have it, George. I'm marking my calendar right now."

They summarize a specific plan and propose follow-up.

STANLEY: "Great, Tom. I'll look forward to talking with you about it. What else did you want to talk about today?"

BURKE: "While we're on the subject of productivity, I have been having more and more trouble keeping my department's productivity up with the heavy workload. A number of other supervisors have been coming to me with technical questions, and they're eating up huge chunks of my time. I just can't drop everything and help them out every time they come around with a problem."

STANLEY: "You sound pretty exasperated, Tom. I gather that you're concerned with your working relationship with the other supervisors."

BURKE: "Yea, they're acting like a bunch of jerks. They will hardly talk to me anymore. I tried to apologize to Kay Drake about a mix-up in communication, but she wouldn't accept my apology."

STANLEY: "You don't sound very happy about that."

BURKE: "Well, I'm not. It really bugs me when the deadwood around here just leans on me."

STANLEY: "Pretty frustrating situation, that's for sure."

BURKE: "I think we should fire the whole bunch of them!"

STANLEY: "It seems as though you're about at the end of your rope."

BURKE: "Well, I am. I just don't know what else can be done. I'm under tremendous pressure to maintain my department's productivity, and yet the other supervisors want me to help them out, too."

STANLEY: "So you feel in conflict, Tom. Either you keep up your productivity or you help out in other departments. Let's start at the beginning. Give me your view of what has happened between you and the other supervisors in the last year. Let's begin with when and how you began cutting back on the amount of help you gave them."

Stanley acknowledges Burke's strong feelings and gets to the core of the problem first, and then begins probing with a "how" question.

BURKE: "As you know, I've always been pretty good technically, and before I became a supervisor, I used to consult with several supervisors on technical problems. After I became a supervisor, they continued to come to me for technical help. For the first year I spent a lot of time with them, but my own work started piling up. I never thought this new job would demand so much of my time. So I cut back on the help I gave them."

STANLEY: "I see. And how did you cut back?"

BURKE: "I just stopped helping them out. I cut way back on returning phone calls and put them off when they came over to see me."

STANLEY: "How did you decide to do it that way?"

BURKE: "I was really concerned and thought it was best to make the break quickly."

STANLEY: "I gather that you decided not to talk with them or me before making the break. How well has this method worked out for you?"

BURKE: "Well, they weren't too happy about it, and some hard feelings have developed on both sides. That's about where it stands now."

STANLEY: "I appreciate your honesty, Tom. You mentioned that problem with Kay Drake a minute ago."

BURKE: "Oh, that. That was just an oversight on my part. I just forgot to get back to Kay; it was purely unintentional. But she took it the wrong way, and I got labeled as a lone wolf again."

STANLEY: "I'm glad to hear that you didn't do it intentionally, Tom. As you look back at your relationship with the other supervisors, what might you have done differently?"

BURKE: "I think I would have explained to them why I pulled back."

STANLEY: "I think that would have helped a lot, Tom. Maybe we could have a meeting and hash all of this out."

BURKE: "Sounds good to me. There's a lot of room for improvement."

STANLEY: "In fact, we all probably keep to ourselves more than we should. Let's try a Monday morning supervisors' meeting each week for two months to see if we can

improve communication throughout the section. We could
use the meetings to make plans for joint efforts on work
for each week. We might also work out a schedule for
weekly job assignments."

BURKE: "Oh, I thought you'd bring that up today."

STANLEY: "Yes, I want to discuss it with you, Tom. On
a couple of occasions you have turned down assignments.
What was your thinking at the time?"

After summing up a plan for improving communication and
relationships among the supervisors, Stanley brings up a problem—
but not in a threatening way.

BURKE: "They were routine jobs that any supervisor in the
section could handle. It seems fair to me that the most
productive group in the section should get the most interesting assignments."

STANLEY: "Let's consider that for a minute, Tom. If I
give your group the most interesting and challenging assignments, how am I going challenge and stimulate the
other groups?"

BURKE: "I don't think they're up to the challenge. Right
now, they bring the most difficult work to me, so I end
up doing the work anyway. You might as well assign it
to me directly."

STANLEY: "But you've already said that you're overloaded,
Tom. Your group can't take on all the difficult jobs in
the section."

BURKE: "No, not all of them."

Burke and Stanley disagree, but neither is lecturing or threatening the other.

STANLEY: "I need to make my position clear, Tom. I need
to follow a fair system of assigning work to each group.
I simply cannot give you the most interesting work in
the section. Favoring your group would hurt morale and
also contributes nothing to the development of technical

expertise in other groups. As I said before, we can work out job assignments in our weekly meetings. At least then we can try to accommodate your preferences as well as everybody else's.

Stanley does some telling in a straightforward and reasonable way.

BURKE: "We can at least give it a try."

STANLEY: "We'll do that, and then review the method of assignment after two months. To summarize, then, we have a plan to hold weekly meetings to promote more communication and cooperation between groups and to work out job assignments. You also set the goal of considering which of your employees can be rotated within your department or elsewhere in the section to reduce turnover. Is there anything else you wish to discuss?"

BURKE: "No. That covers my agenda for today. I think we have a good plan to keep my turnover down, and I'm looking forward to spending more time training my staff. I'm also relieved that the hard feelings between me and the other supervisors came up in our discussion. I'd like to clear the air."

STANLEY: "I'm glad you feel that way, Tom. We'll keep in touch about the progress of our weekly meetings and the turnover in your department. I really appreciate your suggestions during our discussion today."

Burke and Stanley have had a productive and non-threatening interview. They discussed all the topics in the case without defensiveness or lecturing.

Counseling
Interviewing

——————————————————4

Virtually all of us have at times struggled with a problem we were unable to solve ourselves and have turned to someone else for help. Often we may not have even been able to say with any precision what the problem was, but we knew we had strong feelings of frustration, pain, anger, or anxiety. This turning to another for help leads to a counseling interview. A counseling interview is a discussion between two people in which one is asking the other for assistance with a problem or predicament.

Of all the interviews addressed in this book, the counseling interview is most likely to be unplanned and unstructured, and it probably requires the highest degree of sensitivity from the interviewer. Indeed, we may not even know when we are likely to enter into such an interview. Several years ago after the first day of a two-day managerial training course I was conducting, the senior manager of the group asked if he and I could meet for dinner. I assumed that he was going to discuss how the course was going, but a couple of minutes after we sat down, he began to speak of how unhappy he was in his current job and of his deep concern about the career he had chosen. I found myself in the role of a counselor. Really, the counseling interview is best defined by the roles two people assume — one is willing to open up and reveal feelings and problems, and the other is willing to listen and try to help.

It is important to note that most people who assume the role of counselor are not professionally trained. Social workers, psychologists, and psychiatrists are all experts in the helping professions. They counsel people who have serious personality problems or who have major difficulties coping with everyday life. Most of you who are reading this chapter, however, are *part-time* counselors, just as I was when the manager invited me to dinner. As such, you must be aware of your limitations as well as your capabilities and responsibilities.[1] There is much that you can do as a part-time counselor, but you must know when you are over your head and need to refer the person to a professional.

The distinction between part-time and professional counseling is determined by two factors: the setting in which the problem originates and the nature of the problem. While these two factors are clearly related, let's consider them one at a time. The setting of problems addressed in the counseling interview by managers, supervisors, and peers is the workplace. The problems are generally work-related, such as matters of performance on the job, job or career choice, compatibility in a work group, or working conditions (travel, long hours). These are clearly work-related matters that may be appropriately discussed by another employee assuming the role of part-time counselor. Problems whose primary setting is outside of work, such as personal problems, are best left to professional counselors.

There are problems that have their roots outside the work setting but strongly influence job performance. Personal crises such as marital difficulties, financial stress, or substance abuse are examples. Should the part-time counselor get involved with such problems that span both the work and the home settings? Here is where the nature of the problem becomes the determining factor. Consider the instance where the wife's recent promotion conflicts with a planned transfer that will keep the husband on the fast track of career development. This problem, while involving both work and home life, could be addressed effectively in a counseling interview by many managers. On the other hand, more severe personal crises such a marital separation or substance abuse are likely beyond the expertise of even the most skillful part-time counselor and should therefore be referred to a professional. The human resource department or an employee assistance program is an excellent source of help for employees with such problems.

HELP IS A SCARCE COMMODITY

Many observers have concluded that help from a fellow human being is scarce these days. There is a reluctance for people to "get involved" in the personal business of others. We are often prone to shy away from people who are behaving unusually or appear distressed. We feel that we may be intruding.

On the other hand, those who are feeling the distress may wonder why no one takes notice. They may conclude that nobody cares enough about them to inquire and try to help. People often cry out for help in subtle or indirect ways. Many of us either do not detect the signals that people use to ask for help or we choose to ignore them.

Risks of Asking for Help

One of the reasons that people do not ask for help more directly is in part a function of our North American culture. This is particularly true in the business world.[2] Competence is highly valued in most organizations, as well it should be. But this emphasis on competence can be so strong that employees feel it is a liability for them not to have all the answers. How risky is it for a middle manager with 20 years of experience to admit to a work-related problem? Can the fast-track MBA afford to reveal concern over a career choice?

Whether employees in an organization can freely ask their peers or managers for help depends on two factors. The first is the culture of the organization, which is manifested in the way any given peer or manager views another person's request for help. Does one employee see another's request as a constructive step or an admission of weakness? The current emphasis on quality and teamwork has created a positive culture more conducive to employee counseling because employees are encouraged to identify problems openly and try to solve them with the help of others.

The second factor is the skill of the people who conduct counseling interviews. This is probably more important than the first factor. How the counseling is actually done says much more to employees than the unwritten culture of the organization or a manager's announced views. We have all known managers who claimed that the door was always open, but they were so insensitive or unskillful in dealing with employee problems that no one ventured through the door more than once.

Ways in Which the Counseling Interview Can Arise

A counseling interview can arise in two basic ways. The most common is the way already described and illustrated. Someone comes to you and asks for assistance or expresses strong negative feelings, and then you begin to help the person define the problem more clearly.

It is also possible for the counselor to initiate the counseling interview. This type of interview will commonly be triggered when you detect a change in the behavior or job performance of an employee and offer to discuss the matter and try to help. A counseling interview is appropriate when the change is not extreme enough to require disciplinary action (see Chapter 6). You should initiate the interview by commenting specifically on the change and then expressing your willingness to talk, if the employee wants to. This approach is risky, however, and requires a great deal of sensitivity from the counselor. You should try it only with employees with whom you have a good working relationship. (Some specific examples of how you can initiate a counseling interview in this way are given later in the chapter.)

In this chapter I will provide guidance in how to conduct effective counseling interviews. Much of the emphasis will be on what the counselor must do, but I have included several techniques and illustrations that will also guide the client—the person who is seeking help.

OBJECTIVES

As was stated earlier, the counseling interview is usually unplanned and unscheduled. What begins as a casual conversation or a discussion of another matter may evolve into a counseling interview. The fact that it is unplanned, however, does not mean that it has to be unstructured. As prospective counselors, you need to know the content of the typical counseling interview to conduct this type of interview effectively when the need arises. As always, we will begin our discussion of content with objectives. They are:

1. *Problem definition*—Promote maximum flow of information from the client to define the problem and identify potential causes.

2. *Problem solving*—Consider alternative solutions.

3. *Action planning*—Select a course of action endorsed by the client and counselor.

4. *Assigning responsibility for action*—Clarify the client's commitment to change and ensure follow-up.

There are some fundamental points about these objectives that are crucial to effective counseling interviewing. First, you must address these objectives in order. A problem cannot be solved until it has been defined. While this point is obvious, there are many traps that you can fall into that shift the interview to problem solving and even action planning before the problem has been clearly defined by the client. One common example is that many of us, when presented with a matter that is troubling a friend or acquaintance, want to relieve that person's discomfort as quickly as possible. We may also feel a strong urge to reduce our own discomfort, which develops when someone we care about is suffering. Consequently, we rush to a solution for the problem as we perceive it. This solution, however, may be premature or even inappropriate. Furthermore, if the client accepts our solution and carries it out unsuccessfully, the client may hold us responsible for the failure.

A second fundamental point about these objectives is that all of them must be achieved for the client to reap the most benefit possible from the interview. Many counseling interviewers complete only the first two objectives and perhaps a portion of the third. While it is true that some people face more problems than others, it is also true that some people seem always to be unhappy and are continually struggling with some form of problem. You need to be on your guard for this kind of client because he or she can waste a great deal of your time. Such clients often avoid addressing all four objectives in a counseling interview. Some are primarily interested in discussing and complaining about their problems and will drink in all the understanding and sympathy you can muster, but they will avoid attempts to consider alternative solutions. Others may discuss and reject every conceivable solution and never set out specific plans to solve the problem. Still others will not accept responsibility for the proposed course of action but, rather, will press you for a solution and, if it is not successful, will blame you. You need a high degree of skill to avoid falling into the traps that clients may set either deliberately or unintentionally.

INTERACTION OF COUNSELOR AND CLIENT

In the interview, the counselor and client interact, and consequently each influences the behavior of the other. Each has basic values and feelings that contribute to his or her perceptions of the specific problem under discussion and the counseling interview in general. This interaction is shown in Figure 4.1.

The interaction of these feelings, values, and perceptions will strongly influence the approach taken in the interview and its eventual outcome. I alluded earlier to the cultural value that people who seek help are weak. Managers who subscribe to this value may develop strong negative feelings toward a client. Feelings of annoyance or even contempt may arise in these managers when their help is sought. They may also experience conflicting feelings if a person whom they hold in very high regard appears in the office and reveals a problem he or she cannot solve alone. Managers in these circumstances may deny the existence of the problem or try to come up with a quick solution to escape from such an uncomfortable situation.

Other people who are called upon to conduct counseling interviews may place a high value on helping others. Earlier in

Figure 4.1
INTERACTION OF COUNSELOR AND CLIENT

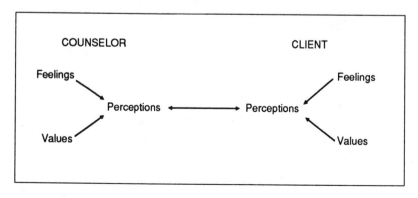

this chapter I gave the example of people who gain great satisfaction from reducing the discomfort of someone who is wrestling with a problem. As counselors, these people may identify very strongly with the client's problem even before it is defined and rush to a solution by giving advice. In workshops I have encountered many managers who try to solve an employee's problem too quickly because their job requires them to solve technical and staff problems routinely. After quickly giving their advice they may leave the interview with a warm glow of satisfaction, but the client's problem may not have been addressed thoroughly.

Of course, the client's feelings and values also strongly influence the way in which the counseling interview is conducted and its outcome. Clients frequently have strong feelings of fear, frustration, or anger that distort their perceptions of the problem and its potential solutions. As counselors, you need to use various skills and techniques to deal with these feelings and perceptions, as will be discussed later in the chapter. Clients may also subscribe to the value that seeking help is a sign of weakness and may therefore feel in conflict when they actually ask you for help. They may be fearful and embarrassed but also sufficiently concerned about their circumstances to ask for help. As a result of this conflict, they may not be very open in the interview, showing a reluctance to own up to the problem or to give all their views and feelings. You will need to deal with this reluctance effectively if the interview is to succeed.

Approach

Now let's turn to approach. Certainly the interaction of the counselor and client and the role that each assumes in the interview will determine how the interview can be approached and conducted. But you must strive to develop an approach that will not be restricted by the client's behavior. Your approach must be flexible enough to adjust to the client as well as to the problem under discussion.

Probably the most common approach to the counseling interview is that advocated by Carl Rogers in client-centered therapy, that is, the nondirective approach.[3] In its purest form the nondirective approach involves the counselor's acting as a mirror to a client. He or she reflects the ideas or content of what the client is saying as well as the feelings that the client is expressing. The primary objective of the nondirective counselor is to help clients gain awareness of their own ideas and feelings regarding a problem. Armed with this awareness, clients then proceed to gain insight and solve their own problems.

At the other end of the continuum is the directive approach. Here the counselor diagnoses the client's problem with minimal assistance from the client and gives advice to alleviate the problem. Although the directive approach is seldom seen in a pure form, it is most likely to occur when there is a large difference in status and power between the client and counselor. Highly directive approaches are common between parent and child, teacher and student, and even manager and employee.

Neither extreme—directive or nondirective—is appropriate in the counseling interview. Rather, as counselors you must tailor your approach to your clients as well as to yourselves. Most significantly, you must tailor your approach to the objective you are dealing with in the interview.[4]

Begin with a nondirective approach. The first objective— problem definition—requires a nondirective approach (Table 4.1). It is imperative that you listen, probe, paraphrase ideas, and reflect feelings to keep the lines of communication wide open during the initial stage of the interview. It is difficult, however, for some counselors to remain nondirective until the problem has been well defined. Instead, they are prone to give in to their own needs by rushing to a premature solution to save time or to relieve their own discomfort or that of the client. It is necessary for you to resist these needs and maintain a nondirective approach until the client has defined the problem clearly and completely.

Table 4.1
CONDUCTING THE COUNSELING INTERVIEW

I. **During the Interview**

    A. Listen actively; look for points to follow **NONDIRECTIVE**
        up on

    B. Head nod, Um huh, Encouraging words

    C. Watch for feelings and reflect them

    D. Paraphrase ideas

    E. Summarize key themes

    F. Ask specific probes: How, Why, How well,
        Do differently?

    G. Ask the client to consider alternatives

    H. Encourage the client to make choices

    I.   Encourage the client to make plans
                                        DIRECTIVE

II. **Information-Collecting Sequence**

    A. **INITIATE** — Initiate the discussion with open-ended questions
                    about the client's problem

    B. **LISTEN** — Listen for underlying themes in the client's com-
                    ments that you will pursue

    C. **FOCUS** — Focus on specific topics the client raises

    D. **PROBE** — Ask how, why, how well, and do differently as
                    you examine the client's comments about the nature
                    of the problem, its symptoms, and its causes

    E. **USE** — Use the discussion to help the client set plans
                    to solve the problem

Strict adherence to the nondirective approach beyond the point of problem definition, however, can be not only annoying to the client, but also unproductive. A manager in one of my workshops on employee counseling once demonstrated this point in an exercise. He was practicing counseling techniques with a fellow participant serving as a client. She posed a work-related problem that she had been thinking about and wrestling with for several days, but after she clearly and concisely defined the problem, the manager continued to paraphrase and summarize what she had already said. Finally in frustration she said, "Don't give me all that nondirective stuff. I have defined the problem clearly; what I need from you is ideas!"

Become more directive as the interview progresses. The objectives of problem solving, action planning, and assigning responsibility for action require you to give a combination of nondirective and directive responses. In general, you will need to become more directive when addressing these three objectives than when dealing with the first objective—problem definition. For example, you must help the client focus on important topics. This may require you to point out central themes in what the client has been saying and to focus the client's attention on these themes. You may also become more directive by contributing your own suggestions for solutions for the client to consider before the client chooses a course of action and turns to action planning. Finally, you may need to be directive to keep the client moving through all four objectives, as illustrated in the last section of this chapter.

Format

The counseling interview is the most spontaneous and least structured of all the interviews addressed in this book. In spite of this, it has a basic format that you should follow as you find yourselves in a counseling situation. Here is the format.

Keep the client talking. The client will trigger the beginning of the counseling interview by asking for assistance or by revealing some need for assistance. As the counselor, your emphasis early in the interview is to keep the lines of communication wide open and to keep the client talking about the nature of the problem. Using nondirective techniques such as paraphrasing ideas, reflecting feelings, summarizing, and asking specific questions will keep the information flowing.

Encourage the client to consider alternative solutions. After the problem and its potential causes have been identified, your next step is to encourage the client to begin helping himself or herself. What solutions have been tried? What ideas have been considered and discarded? Here you are essentially getting the client to think aloud and consider what is possible.

Add your own ideas. As you and the client progress in the problem-solving stage of the interview, you may wish to offer your own alternatives for the client's consideration. You should do so cautiously and only *after* you have exhausted the client's own ideas.

Set specific plans. At this stage of the interview, you must help the client plan for the future. Some clients may do this automatically; others will need encouragement and direction from you. First, the client must select from among the alternatives identified in the previous two steps. Second, he or she must set out a specific plan of action that will lead to a desired change in the current predicament. You may have to use some specific questions to get the client to begin planning. "I think you have your options well in mind. What do you plan to do?" or "I think it's important that you proceed with a plan. What would you like to do next?" are good examples.

Gain client commitment to change and propose follow-up. Many of us have had thought-provoking, constructive discussions with a co-worker or manager, and after several months, no one followed up so nothing came of our discussion. Before you end the counseling interview, you and the client need to agree on who is responsible for carrying out the plan, and who will do what, by when, to resolve the problem. This is the way to make change. As the counselor, you need to begin by ensuring that the client clearly perceives his or her responsibility in bringing about change. In many cases individuals contribute to their own difficulties either by behaving in ways that are directly harmful to themselves or by failing to act in ways that would rid them of their difficulties. We all contribute somewhat to our own problems, even if it is just by remaining in the situation that we find problematic. Consequently, we must act in order to solve our problems, for they are seldom resolved by the actions of others. As counselors, you must ensure that the client is aware of and accepts his or her responsibility to carry out the plans for change to see that change does indeed occur.

A Note of Caution

Early in this chapter I stressed the distinction between professional counselors and the rest of us who venture into counseling only at the invitation of someone with whom we work or live, or when we choose to initiate a discussion of a work-related problem or a personal problem affecting work. As part-time counselors, you must be aware of your limitations. In particular, you must be on the lookout for problems that you have neither the knowledge nor the skill to address effectively.

Turning to the format just discussed, after you have completed the first step and done your best to help the client define the problem, ask yourself, "Can I help with this problem?"

For example, if one of your best employees has just traced his decrease in job performance to a marital or substance abuse problem, you're probably in over your head. While you may have great concern for the employee's well-being and strong views on the reasons for his or her difficulties, you are very likely not the best person to serve as his counselor. It is important that you realize this immediately after defining the problem rather than after you have struggled further into the interview. You should state clearly that you appreciate the employee's candor and that you feel he or she needs more expert help than you can give. Your problem solving should then focus on identifying a more appropriate source of help for the client, such as your organization's Employee Assistance Plan or the Human Resource Department.

CONDUCTING THE COUNSELING INTERVIEW

Now that we have set out a format to meet the objectives of the counseling interview, let's turn to the techniques for conducting this kind of interview. The counseling interview is different from the other four interview types discussed in this book. In each of the other four, interviewers have a set of objectives, a format, and an agenda of topics they wish to cover. As counseling interviewers, you also have objectives and a format, but you have no planned agenda of topics. Consequently, in the counseling interview you must work exclusively with the material raised by the client. To use what the client is saying as effectively as possible, you must rely heavily on the sequence of initiate-listen-focus-probe-use (Table 4.1). Following this sequence will help you to minimize the influence of your own views in the counseling interview and to maintain a predominantly nondirective approach. Let's consider this sequence in more detail.

Initiate. As noted earlier in this chapter, there are two ways in which to initiate a counseling interview. The first is for the manager, supervisor, or colleague of the prospective client to take the initiative by assuming the role of the counseling interviewer and inviting the other person to assume the role of the client. Initiating the interview is risky and requires that the counselor have a good relationship with the other person. You can begin by describing the changes you have observed in the individual's behavior and then express your willingness to help. For example,

> COUNSELOR: "I've noticed a change in your working hours in the last couple of weeks. You are usually the first one here in the morning and one of the last to leave, but lately you've been coming in later and leaving earlier than I've seen you do in the five years you've been in the department. I just wanted you to know that if there's anything you'd like to talk over with me, I'm here to listen."

> CLIENT: "Well, I have been stewing about something and I guess it shows. Do you remember that promotion to the Sales Department that I applied for? They turned me down and brought in somebody with far less experience from outside the company."

It is very important to be specific when describing the change and to avoid any evaluation of the behavior. Vague, judgmental generalities (for example, "You've been slacking off on your working hours lately; what's wrong with you anyway?") will only make the employee defensive.

The second and more common way to initiate a counseling interview is to respond to another employee's request for assistance or expression of negative feelings. Here you are responding to a prospective client's direct or subtle invitation to assume the role of counselor. Sometimes the invitation is quite straightforward, as in the following example.

> CLIENT: "I'd like to talk with you about transferring to another department. I've been thinking it over for quite some time, and I'd really appreciate your thoughts."

> COUNSELOR: "Sure, I'd be glad to talk about it. Can you start at the beginning?"

Frequently, however, the call for help is indirect. In these cases you have to be quite sensitive to the feelings that accompany the employee's words, and, if you sense a good deal of distress, reflect the feelings. For example,

> CLIENT: "It really bugs me when the new fast-track employees get the most challenging assignments."

> COUNSELOR: "You sound pretty frustrated about it."

> CLIENT: "I am. I've got a lot more experience than those kids. Maybe I should update my résumé and find some place where management values knowledgeable employees."

> COUNSELOR: "It sounds like you're about at the end of your rope. Would you like to talk about it?"

CLIENT: "Sure. I don't really want to leave, but I will if I don't start getting some of the tough projects around here. I'm glad someone in the department cares about how I feel."

In this example, the "client" is clearly exasperated and is considering rather drastic action. Reflecting strong feelings and offering to listen is the first step in what may become a counseling interview.

Once you have initiated a counseling interview in either of the two ways described, it may proceed for just a few minutes or for more than an hour. You simply must follow the client's lead. You cannot counsel someone who is unwilling to open up and talk. But, given a responsive client, there is much that you can do to make the interview successful.

Listen. While it is essential that you listen carefully throughout the counseling interview, listening is particularly important during the first stage of the interview directed toward problem definition. Watch for strong feelings in facial expressions or tone of voice as well as the ideas the feelings accompany. You will need to deal with the feelings first, before going into the actual ideas the client is conveying.

Focus and Probe. There are a number of ways in which you can respond to what the client says, but each response should be aimed at keeping the channels of communication open. As you listen to the client, you will need to store points that you will turn to later by focusing on them and probing for more detail. In the counseling interview you must pay special attention to how your responses affect the client and the communication flow. The following example illustrates this point.

Consider yourself talking with a woman in her late twenties who is currently employed as an accountant. You are the manager of the department and during a visit to your office she says the following:

"I've been in this office for three years now—and in the same department for two years—but I hardly know anybody in the department. I just can't seem to make friends. I just freeze up—I try to be nice to the clerical staff and the other accountants, but I feel all stiff and uncomfortable inside. And then I tell myself that I don't care. People aren't dependable. Everyone is out for himself. I don't want any friends—and sometimes I think I really mean that."

This employee is obviously feeling alone and frustrated and is very openly asking for help. Your role as a counselor is to respond to what she has said and enter into a counseling interview. The following five responses are illustrations of five different types of responses that you could give. Read them carefully and choose the ones that you think are the most appropriate.

1. "Well, I'll tell you what I can do. I can arrange for you to join a special interest group in the office. I have given that advice to quite a few people who have difficulty in making friends. Most start out attending discussion programs, coffee hours, lectures, or some other program. This gives them something to get interested in and an opportunity to make friends slowly and at their own pace."

2. "Could you tell me a little more about how you go about trying to make friends so we could get a clearer idea of what is involved?"

3. "It's gone on so long it almost has you convinced—is that what you mean?"

4. "Maybe your not wanting friends is just to protect you from something else?"

5. "That's a pretty unhappy situation, to be without friends, and one that I would really work on. There are a number of things that you might do to learn how to make friends and the sooner you start, the better."

1. *Solution*. Examine each response in detail. The first is clearly a solution, and as such it is premature. The manager has reached into a drawer and pulled out a quick solution before the problem has been defined. This suggestion may indeed be appropriate and useful to the accountant, but the manager should not offer it until after the problem has been explored and defined.

A word of caution here. There are fundamental reasons why counselors give a quick solution to a client. Some do so in an attempt to reduce the discomfort that the problem causes either them or their client. It's a relief to all concerned to have the problem solved quickly. In addition, when there is a clear difference in power or status between the counselor and client, some counselors are prone to jump to a quick solution. People in positions of authority, such as managers, teachers, and parents, must be particularly mindful of suspending judgment and withholding solutions until they have allowed the client to define the problem and generate some alternative solutions to be considered.

The counselor who gives a quick solution runs still another risk. The counseling interview ends ideally when the client produces the solution. Clients are generally more committed to solutions they work out themselves, and they are more likely to recognize their own responsibility in making the solution work. If your suggestion to the client is not effective, you may find yourself bearing the blame for its failure.

2. *Question*. The next response in the illustration is a very useful open-ended question that asks the client to add some information that may reveal a potential cause of her frustration. It focuses on one particular element of what she has expressed—how she tries to make friends—and then probes for more detail.

The probing sequence recommended in performance appraisal interviews is also appropriate in the counseling interview (Table 4.1). After asking *how* the accountant tries to make friends, you could follow up with *why* she does it that way, *how well* it works out for her, and whether she has ideas of how she would *do it differently* in the future.

3. *Show understanding.* In this response, the counselor shows some understanding of the predicament by reflecting the mixture of frustration and futility the client is expressing. By reflecting these feelings, the counselor is focusing on a specific element of the client's initial statement and is encouraging her to elaborate on her feelings.

The second and third types of responses are most useful at this stage of the counseling interview because they keep the lines of communication wide open and encourage the client to define the problem.

4. *Interpretation.* This response is inappropriate. In making this comment, the counselor is assuming the role of amateur psychiatrist and is interpreting the client's behavior in terms of an underlying psychological cause. Such a response is not useful in a counseling interview for two reasons. First, a part-time counselor is very likely unqualified to make a psychological diagnosis, especially on such limited information. Second, such a response is very unlikely to be useful to the client or to the progress of the counseling interview. It may make her feel defensive. It may frighten her. It will almost certainly reduce the flow of communication between herself and the counselor.

5. *Evaluation.* In this response, the counselor is using personal values to judge the severity of the client's predicament. In the counselor's view, being without friends is an unhappy situation that needs urgent attention. Indeed, most people would agree. But the *timing* of such an evaluation is the important matter here. It has come much too early in the interview. The client may have many friends outside work. She may come to realize that the reason she has not become friends with her colleagues at work is that she finds little in common with them or dislikes her chosen line of work. While the counselor's intention in making this statement may be to motivate the client, it can backfire. As a counselor,

you should make evaluative statements only when the client is weighing alternatives and needs your direction.

In focusing and probing in the counseling interview, you need to remain as neutral as possible as you seek to help the client define the problem. In each of the three inappropriate responses—solution, interpretation, and evaluation—the counselor was responding to personal values and needs as well as to the client's need for assistance. You have to work very hard as a counselor to ignore your own needs and values and focus on the need of the client to define the problem, consider alternatives, and develop a plan for change.

Use. The last step in the sequence of initiate-listen-focus-probe-use is of particular importance in the counseling interview. The most effective counseling interview will not end until the client has set a plan of action, is clearly committed to that plan, and follow-up has been ensured. As a counselor, you have the responsibility of helping the client use what has been discussed earlier in the interview to set plans and goals. Consequently, you need to direct the client's attention toward the future with comments such as the following:

> "I think we've reached a pretty clear understanding of what has been troubling you. What do you think you can do to change the situation?"

>   or

> "You seem quite motivated to work your way out of this dilemma. What steps are open to you?"

You may have an opportunity to give your views on the feasibility of various alternatives in this final stage of the interview. You may wish to evaluate the planning that the client is doing, or you may even offer your own solutions. How directive you become depends largely on how much the client appears to be receptive to your ideas or whether the client even openly asks for them. I recommend that you follow the client's lead and, when offering a solution, put it in the form of a proposal for the client to consider. For example,

"I've got an idea that I'd like to try out on you. Would it be possible for you to...?"

or

"As we talked this whole situation through, I've come up with an idea that I'd like you to think about. What do you think of the possibility of...?"

It is generally desirable to withhold your own views until after you have sought out the perceptions and proposals of the client. And when you make your proposals in the form of the examples given, you are giving the client a choice, not a guaranteed solution. This will ensure that the client accepts responsibility for the plans that are worked out in the counseling interview. On the other hand, if you give strong advice or promote a specific solution, you run the risk of accepting responsibility for the solution. If it fails, the client may blame you.

MANAGING THE COUNSELING INTERVIEW

The counseling interview demands much of you as an interviewer. Although you have a set of objectives and a format, you do not enter the interview with content that you have worked out prior to the interview. Indeed, you may not even be aware that you have entered a counseling interview until you are in one. And yet, once you find yourself in a counseling interview, it is your responsibility to run it effectively. This will require you to draw heavily on fundamental interviewing techniques to manage this type of interview.

Managing the interview involves two basic functions. The first is to draw out central themes and ideas from what you hear the client saying. This is similar to putting a jigsaw puzzle together.

Many clients have not thought their situations through thoroughly, and so they give you a relatively disorganized combination of symptoms, perceptions, feelings, and proposals. Your challenge is to integrate what you hear and feed it back in a more organized way. This is hard work that takes a good deal of ability to think conceptually. But you have the advantage of hearing for the first time what has been whirling around in the client's mind for weeks or even months. Listen very carefully, focusing and probing with the techniques discussed earlier in this chapter. Then periodically summarize the emerging themes.

Your second function in managing counseling interviews is to keep clients moving through your format so that you can meet all four objectives in the interview. First, you need to keep clients from repeating themselves by drawing their attention to central themes that emerge in the interview. Second, you need to keep them moving from problem definition to problem solving and from problem solving to planning. Sometimes this may require a gentle nudge. You may have to turn their attention by asking future-oriented questions, such as:

"I think we both understand your predicament pretty well. Now, let's think about what your options are."

or

"I think we have a good list of options. Which one appears most promising to you?"

or

"It's clear to me that you want to change jobs. I think it's important that you develop a plan of action to meet this goal. Let's see if we can work out a detailed strategy."

If you are able to manage the counseling interview in this way, both you and your client can succeed in meeting your respective needs. You will assist the client in meeting his or her need for help, and you will find yourself in the company of a less distressed companion.

Career Planning Interviewing

---5

We have entered an era in which many people are seeking careers, rather than "just a job." In this era of heightened career orientation, people have developed high expectations for personal growth and self-fulfillment in their work lives. Sometimes these expectations can be unrealistically high, especially among recent graduates with bachelors or masters degrees who enter an organization with the naive view that they can rise in their careers in a very short period of time. These expectations for a work life that is not only materially rewarding, but also personally fulfilling, whether realistic or not, have spawned a desire among employees to manage their own careers. They want to know where they are headed in their work lives and how each work assignment or job they take fits into an overall plan of career development. They are particularly interested in learning as much as possible from each job and each employer as they strive to grow in their work. The steps that individuals take to identify and achieve their career goals is *career planning*. To put it bluntly, many employees seem today to be at least as interested in what their employer can do for them as they are in what they can do for their employer.

Of course, self-interest has always been common among employees. Fundamentally, we all work for ourselves first, and since our performance usually contributes to the goals of our employer, both parties benefit. It does appear, however, that some of the unwritten rules governing employee behavior have changed during this era of heightened career orientation. Employees appear less strongly committed to their employers, in part because of decreasing job security resulting from the spate of takeovers and acquisitions during the 1980s.[1] They are less willing to transfer. They change jobs and employers more often than in the past. Some of you may remember when turnover was considered a sign of instability in people, and having changed jobs more than two or three times in a five-year period was viewed negatively. Today, this level of turnover is likely to be viewed as a positive sign of upward mobility and career development!

As a manager responsible for the job performance of your employees, you can expect to be affected by their strong desire to plan and develop their own careers. You will probably be influenced from two directions. New employees will look to you for information and guidance as they plan their own careers. In addition, your boss or the human resource department of your company may expect you to take a more active role in *career management*—the steps the organization takes to provide a pool of qualified people to meet future needs. In recent years, organizations have instituted many new programs to assist employees in career planning and managers in career management.[2] Examples are workshops in which employees assess their own abilities, interests, and values, computerized human resource information systems to assist in developing and promoting current employees, providing information to employees about potential career paths in the organization, and assigning experienced employees to serve as "mentors" who advise and counsel new employees about their career development. How can you respond effectively to these added responsibilities regarding your employees' careers?

The answer to this question is for you to *enter into* the career planning that your employees are already doing. Your task is to help them do a better job of developing their own careers by giving them information and guidance. It is important for you to remember that in career development, what is good for your employees is generally also good for you and your company. Employees who progress to more complex and challenging work assignments or from one job to the next, expanding their potential to perform and increasing their satisfaction with their work, will become more valuable to their organization in the process if they remain with that organization. This leads us to your role as a manager in career planning. If you can help employees develop so that they perform at the top of their potential, and if you can also retain them in the organization, both the employees and your company benefit. The career planning interview is a means of ensuring that this development of employees occurs for the benefit of both the employee and the employer.

In some circumstances, employees can develop their careers only by leaving their current employer. If employee turnover is inevitable, the manager and employee should discuss and plan for such a move openly to ensure that the employee leaves with no bad feelings and to provide information to the manager so that the organization can recognize the lack of opportunity for career development and strive to improve the situation.

DEFINITION OF CAREER PLANNING

Let's have a closer look at career planning. A definition of career planning must begin with a definition of career. Hall[3] defines career as "the individually perceived sequence of attitudes and behaviors associated with work-related experiences and activities over the span of a person's life." There are several conclusions that we can draw from this definition.

First, career is a very personal phenomenon. "Individually perceived" implies that each of us defines his or her own career in his or her own terms. What may appear to someone else to be a very unsuccessful or dissatisfying career may be very satisfying to the individual. A career is not necessarily movement up a promotional ladder. Moving from less difficult to more difficult assignments or simply doing the same type of work in the same job for many years is also a career.[4] Second, career is a life-long sequence or process that develops and unfolds over time. This means that employees of any age and tenure are likely to be concerned with their careers. Third, the term career applies primarily to employees' work lives. While personal matters with a spouse or family may influence career planning, the planning that is done deals primarily with work. Finally, the phrase "attitudes and behaviors" indicates that careers encompass not only what people do, such as performing, earning money, or choosing between jobs, but also how they feel about what they do (satisfied, bored, frustrated, motivated). Often their feelings about their work can be more important to their career planning than what they are actually doing.

Career planning is the process through which one charts, monitors, evaluates, and adjusts one's own career. Career management consists of the steps an organization takes to contribute to the career planning and development of its employees. In a career planning interview, a second party (supervisor, manager, fellow employee, spouse, human resource specialist) assists someone in this process. To clarify the role of the second party who assists someone in career planning, let's return to our definition of career. What must you be aware of as a career planning interviewer?

THE MANAGER'S ROLE
IN CAREER PLANNING

First, as a manager or supervisor, you do career planning *with* someone, not *for* someone. Consequently, the responsibility for career planning is shared by you and the employee. Second, career planning requires you to listen to the other person to learn about perceptions and plans regarding his or her own career. This requires that you collect a good deal of information. Finally, career planning is a dynamic process influenced by new information relating to the employee's work life. Since a career is a life-long process, it is constantly open to evaluation and change. Your role in career planning therefore involves providing work-related information that contributes to the planning process of your employees.

I do not mean to suggest that most people plan their careers and then watch them unfold in a logical and predictable way. For many of us, quite the reverse is true. If we try to trace a logical pattern along the line our career has taken to date, we might be baffled by the sharp twists and turns that occurred. Why did the person who graduated from college with a geography major run his own landscaping and outdoor lighting business for several years and then return to school for a masters degree in social work? Through what tangled trail did a college graduate in geology spend several years on the professional tennis circuit, and then run a very lucrative tennis club, only to take a major cut in income and join a large gas pipeline company in the rates department?

As we look back, we see how we constantly evaluated and reevaluated our career choices as we received and reacted to new information. Remember that how we feel about work-related experiences and activities is an important element of our careers. We receive new information every day that affects our feelings about our work lives. The latest inflation figures suggest to us that we need a job in which we can earn more money. Being passed over for promotion suggests that we're going nowhere in this company. Finishing a project ahead of schedule and receiving recognition from the department head greatly increases commitment to the job and employer.

We are all in a constant state of absorbing new information and re-evaluating our careers. Implicitly or explicitly, we are all in a continuing process of planning our own careers. What does this mean to you as a manager or supervisor who conducts career planning interviews? One of your main responsibilities is to help employees perform as well as they are capable of performing and to retain those employees for as long as they perform well. To do so, you must enter into the career planning process in which your employees are constantly engaged. You need to make this a joint effort while each employee is a member of your organization. You have valuable information that your employees need to plan their careers more effectively. They, in turn, have a wealth of information that you must tap to help them plan their careers in a more informed way. This chapter will help you learn to enter and contribute to the career planning process of your employees in a useful way.

OBJECTIVES

There are four major objectives of a career planning interview. They are

1. Identify satisfactions and dissatisfactions with the current job, career, and employer.
2. Identify employee work needs and goals.
3. Inform the employee of available career paths and developmental opportunities.
4. Formulate a career development plan.

Notice that as the interviewer, you are assuming three distinct roles in the career planning interview. The first two objectives require you to collect information from the employee. The third objective requires you to provide information to the employee. Hence, you must assume the quite different roles of information collector and information giver. Finally, you assume a third role of counselor as you and your employee work together to consider alternatives and make decisions to formulate a career development plan. Assuming three distinct roles to meet four objectives will certainly keep you on your toes in a career planning interview. This degree of complexity requires that you become quite familiar with the objectives you have to address *before* you enter the interview. Let's look at these four objectives in more detail.

Objective 1: Identify satisfactions and dissatisfactions with the current job, career, and employer. It is in pursuit of the first objective that you must learn from your employees and investigate their feelings about their work lives. What characteristics of the work and organization does the employee find particularly satisfying or dissatisfying? What opportunities do the job and the organization offer for development, advancement, and future work satisfaction? You will need to give special attention to:

- nature of the work performed
- what the employee likes and dislikes about the work
- employee's perception of available opportunities for career development inside and outside the organization
- employee's satisfaction with progress to date with his or her career and in the organization.

In this portion of the interview, you need to probe employees' perceptions and feelings about not only their work but also the opportunities the organization offers them to progress in their careers.

Objective 2: Identify employee work needs and goals. The second objective requires you to identify what employees want from their work and how they plan to attain what they want. Of course, every employee will be pursuing somewhat different goals at work, but there are significant similarities among the work needs and goals of employees who are in the same stage of development in their careers.[5] Five *career development stages* are summarized below. I want to emphasize, however, that these stages are not intended as a rigid formula. That is, not everyone in a given stage will have the same needs and goals. This description of the five stages should be used as a general guide. Knowledge of the stages will help you focus more clearly on the issues that are of particular importance to each individual employee and tailor your interview more to the needs of that employee.

1. *Exploration stage.* This is an initial trial period in which individuals discover and experiment with various types of work. Because of limited prior work experience, expectations may be often unrealistically high among employees in this stage. They consider as very important opportunities to advance, to use their unique skills and educational background, to be recognized for their achievements, to be challenged at work and to be paid well. Many face early disappointment, and change jobs and employers frequently in search of the work life that meets their high expectations.

2. *Establishment stage.* Having found a suitable kind of work, employees next turn their attention toward establishing and stabilizing their work lives. Safety and security emerge as important needs as the employees strive to settle down and earn recognition and status in their chosen career through performance.

3. *Advancement stage.* Once employees feel they have found their niche in the work world and have attained sufficient levels of success to feel secure, the desire to create, develop, and advance at work becomes paramount. It is in this stage that we truly become masters of our trade, and ideally develop as far as our intelligence, knowledge, and skills will allow.

4. *Maintenance stage.* This stage spans the greatest portion of our work life from about age 40 to 65 or beyond. Much has been written about the beginning of this career stage, marked by

the entry into the second half of one's life. Terms like "mid-life crisis," "mid-career crisis," and "middle-aged" abound.

About the only valid conclusion concerning this career stage is that it produces tremendously different effects on different people. Some shift into high gear and continue to develop and perform well and reach new heights in their work lives. Others feel that life has passed them by and embark on 25 years of lower work goals and performance, which amounts to stagnation and decline in their work lives. Some observers of careers have characterized these people as acting for 20 years as though they were six months from retirement.

A third group of employees in this career stage have reached their level of competence and maintain that level of performance for another 20 years until retirement. They are the employees who are no longer on the "fast track" of advancement, but can be the backbone of the organization: good, steady, reliable employees. While they look over their shoulders occasionally and see a world of younger people gaining on them, they continue to perform well in areas of work they have mastered.

Finally, there is still another group who enter the maintenance stage but do not remain there long. The maintenance stage does involve a good deal of soul searching, as employees realistically assess their own capabilities, their career choices, and their satisfaction with their work lives. Growing numbers of working people are beginning new careers at mid-life and starting again at the exploration or establishment stage of career development. As the rate of change of the work world continues to increase, technological advances and information booms will force more people either to change careers at least once in their lifetime or to struggle to keep up to date in their first careers. Furthermore, the number of promotions available to the large group of people born between 1946 and 1964 is far too small to satisfy all the baby boomers.[6] Organizations will need to become more creative at satisfying the career development needs of employees in the maintenance stage.

5. *Retirement stage.* The final career stage is one of decline and retirement. At age 60 or later we end our work lives and move into a world of leisure and free time. This is a period of adjustment in which people's energy and goals, albeit declining, must be rechanneled if they are to go on living well and feeling satisfied with life.

Objective 3: Inform the employee of available career paths and developmental opportunities. Your third objective in the career planning interview is to tell employees about what is possible within the organization. Focus the discussion on each available career path, a series of jobs or work assignments through which employees can progress in their careers in the organization. For a clerical employee, a typical career path is receptionist—clerk typist—secretary—administrative assistant—office supervisor. Remember, however, that career development does not necessarily mean being promoted from one job to another. Many employees can develop in their careers while remaining on the same job and taking on more complex and challenging assignments.

Managers also need to look outside their own departments when considering career development opportunities. Many employees move from one department to another in what can be best described as a *career web*, rather than a path. One accountant might aspire to a career path such as accountant—intermediate accountant—senior accountant—supervisor—department manager—controller, while another might move from senior accountant to the auditing department and from there to the quality control department. All these jobs involve the similar functions of organized reporting and control, but in different departments. You will need to do some research in your own and related departments to identify potential career paths and webs for your employees.

In many organizations, employees do not have a very clear understanding of career development opportunities. This is due primarily to lack of information. As I have already said, they need to know the types of work assignments and jobs they can strive for to develop in their careers inside the company. To obtain this information, you will need to look at career development and promotional opportunities not only inside your own department, but also throughout the entire company. In many organizations, the immediate supervisor is not the only person to conduct career planning interviews with an employee. Members of the human resource department or a senior manager acting as a mentor may also become involved in career planning to inform employees of a wider range of career opportunities available in the organization.

But this is just the beginning. Employees must also know how to change their own knowledge and skills so they can prepare themselves to perform successfully in the next work assignment or job in their career paths or webs. Any planning process requires three basic pieces of information: (1) where we are now, (2) where we want to be in the future, and (3) how we get from here to there. Let's translate these fundamental steps into the context of career planning.

1. What are the major responsibilities of my current job?

2. What work assignments or jobs do I aspire to?

3. In what ways do I have to develop as an employee to move from my current job to my desired work assignment or job?

In my years of management consulting, I have seen distressingly few organizations in which there is sufficient information available to employees to answer these three deceptively simple questions. Job descriptions are frequently too general to provide sufficiently detailed information to answer questions 1 and 2 for career planning. Lists of training and development courses are potentially useful in identifying the methods of employee development, but they are most useful only after question 3 has been answered in terms of what the employee must learn to advance to the next work assignment or job.

1. *Work Performance Guides*. In order to know if they can progress to another work assignment or job, employees need to

Figure 5.1
WORK PERFORMANCE REQUIREMENTS

Performance Requirements

Knowledge **"Must Know"**		**Skill** **"Must Be Able** **to Do"**
1. Technical		1. Technical
2. Relational		2. Relational
3. Administrative		3. Administrative
4. Innovative		4. Innovative

Performance Targets
"Make Happen"

1. Technical
2. Relational
3. Administrative
4. Innovative

---

know what they must actually do in that work assignment or job, what knowledge they need, and what skills they must use. This information can be summarized in a "Work Performance Guide," which is a comprehensive job description that I have found to be very useful in career development. I recommend it as a basis for defining the work assignments or jobs in your employees' career paths or webs. Let's take a close look at what is contained in a work performance guide diagrammed in Figure 5.1.

    2. *Performance Targets.* The performance targets specify the job functions for which the employee is responsible. These targets can be broken down into four categories:

Technical—All jobs require that the employee perform a number of technical functions on data, equipment, or things.

Relational—All jobs require that employees deal with others in simple or complex ways.

Administrative—Enforcing or following basic company policies and procedures during the course of the work is a part of all jobs.

Innovative—All jobs require employees to react to the unexpected and develop new ways of doing the work.

The performance targets in these four basic areas clearly identify what an employee must get done on the job. They provide basic information to the process of career planning. Employees looking at a work performance guide for their current job can answer the question, "What am I capable of delivering to this organization? What performance targets can I meet?" Similarly, employees can look at a work assignment or job they aspire to and identify in detail what they must be able to do to make the move. Table 5.1 provides a good illustration of performance targets.

Table 5.1
WORK PERFORMANCE GUIDE

Financial Controls   Treasury Department Job: Assistant Treasurer
Summary of Job Responsibilities
The Assistant Treasurer is primarily responsible for monitoring and maintaining the functions of cash receipts, cash disbursements, payroll, and cash management. He monitors these functions through supervising a banking supervisor and two financial analysts. He also periodically reviews a number of worksheets of the clerical staff and directs the staffing and cross-training of clerical personnel. Finally, he serves as a liaison with other departments in Financial Controls, Company operating departments, and Corporate Accounting, Treasury, and Legal departments.

Performance Targets, Technical

1. *Cash Disbursements.* Monitor the flow of cash disbursements with a regular review, sign checks over $10,000, and periodically review checks of under $10,000. Review and investigate related specific or general procedural problems when they arise and take appropriate action such as (a) make adjustments to respond to fluctuations in the computer schedule and heavy invoice load and (b) as required, make decisions to expedite or postpone certain disbursements.

2. *Cash Receipts.* Monitor the flow of cash receipts to ensure that all receipts have been properly recorded and accounted for by (a) reviewing and approving Daily Statements of Cash Receipts and (b) reviewing monthly reconciliation of cash receipts vouchers to the general ledger.

3. *Cash Management.* Monitor cash management function by (a) reviewing the Daily Wire Transfer Worksheet, (b) reviewing weekly the cash control worksheet, (c) reviewing monthly and weekly cash forecasts, (d) reviewing monthly bank analysis statements, (e) reviewing monthly reconciliation of cash control to the general ledger, and (f) initiating lock box studies in accordance with standard policies and procedures.

4. *Payroll.* Monitor the payroll function to ensure that all employees are paid accurately and timely and that earnings records are maintained in accordance with Employee Relations, Tax, and Operating departmental requirements by (a) reviewing with the banking supervisor that all schedules have been met and (b) reviewing with the banking supervisor and approving vouchers, deduction registers, tax reports, and personnel reports.

Performance Targets, Relational

1. Direct cross-training of Treasury personnel to ensure that each job has a backup by (a) selecting employees to be trained and (b) setting the parameters (content and duration) of the training.

2. Make recommendations to the Treasurer for staffing requirements (RFPs) by reviewing functions, work load, and capability of available personnel.

3. Supervise, direct, and evaluate the work of a banking supervisor and two financial analysts.

4. Through personal contact and written communications, coordinate the flow of required information and reports to and from other Financial Controls departments, all other Company departments, Corporate Treasury, Corporate Legal, and Corporate Financial Controls.

5. Through personal contact and correspondence with various banking reps, monitor the appropriate relationships that the Company has with those banks.

Performance Targets, Administrative

1. Ensure that standard policies, procedures, and internal controls are complied with by (a) informing staff of the policies, procedures, and controls and (b) periodically reviewing checkpoints.

2. Periodically review and revise departmental policies, procedures, and internal controls and, when applicable, recommend changes in Company policies and procedures.

3. Make recommendations to the Treasurer re space, equipment, and systems needs.

Performance Targets, Innovative

1. Keep informed of developments in cash management, accounts payable, accounts receivable, and payroll techniques and principles and, when appropriate, incorporate them into our cash management and payroll systems.

2. Be informed of new techniques and principles in personnel development, supervision, and work and organizational design and recommend appropriate revisions.

3. Develop new policies and procedures and related forms, where needed and practicable.

4. Recognize those situations that involve Treasury, for example, information of a large product purchase or sale, new project, venture or acquisition, and act accordingly.

Knowledge, Technical

Technical knowledge listed applies to the following four areas: (a) cash disbursements, (b) cash receipts, (c) cash management, and (d) payroll.

1. Knowledge of each specific function.

2. Knowledge of Corporate and Company policies and procedures re each function.

3. Knowledge of related Company internal controls.

4. General working knowledge of accounting, finance, banking, computer systems, and company operations.

Knowledge, Relational

1. Knowledge of departmental work flow and capabilities of available staff.
2. Knowledge of training methods.
3. Knowledge of supervisory procedures.
4. Knowledge of needs of other departments for Treasury information and Treasury's needs for information from other departments.
5. Knowledge of organizational structure and who's who within the Company, the Corporate Office, and banks we deal with.
6. Knowledge of company policies and procedures regarding personnel.

Knowledge, Administrative

1. Knowledge of Company and Corporate policies and procedures and internal controls.
2. Knowledge of needs of the department for efficient operations.

Knowledge, Innovative

1. Knowledge of sources of information (trade publications, general business magazines, seminars, personal contact) re cash management, payroll, personnel development, and work and staff supervision.
2. Comprehensive understanding of departmental functions and the policies and procedures affecting them.

Skills, Technical

1. Observational skills.
2. Skill in defining and resolving problems.
3. Diagnostic and analytical skills to find causes of technical problems.

Skills, Relational

1. Supervisory skills.
2. Skills in written and verbal communication.
3. Training skill.
4. Skill to form and maintain good working relationships with staff and also with others not reporting to the Assistant Treasurer.
5. Ability to plan, set priorities, schedule work, and utilize workforce effectively.

Skills, Administrative

1. Ability to analyze, interpret, communicate, and implement standard policies and procedures and internal controls.
2. Ability to diagnose departmental needs for increased efficiency.

Skills, Innovative

1. Ability to recognize need for change.
2. Ability to present new ideas and procedures in a simple and practical way.

3. *Performance Requirements.* Now let's move upward in Figure 5.1. What does it take to meet the performance targets? What is required of the employee? Knowledge and skill combine to produce performance. Both are essential. Consequently, the performance requirements are divided into two basic components:

> *Knowledge*—What the employee must know to achieve the performance targets.

> *Skill*—What the employee must be able to do to achieve the performance targets.

Each of these two performance requirements is divided into the same four categories that apply to performance targets: *technical, relational, administrative,* and *innovative.*

The example in Table 5.1 provides specific examples of knowledge and skill required to achieve performance targets. Notice that while new recruits can be expected to bring some basic knowledge to the job from their educational background, much of the knowledge must be learned after employment begins. If you expect employees to perform their own jobs well or move to other work assignments or jobs in the organization, you must give them opportunities to increase their knowledge and skill through your company's programs of employee development and career planning.

Objective 4: Formulate a Career Development Plan. In the fourth objective of the career planning interview, you need to address the last question in any planning process: how do I get from here to there? In the previous objectives you and the employee have established what the employee wants and what work assignments and jobs the organization can offer. In this final objective, you must identify the opportunities for employee development that will bridge the gap between where the employee is now and where he or she would like to be.

While each individual employee's career development plan is unique, some generalizations can be made about the kind of planning that is appropriate for employees at various stages of their careers. I have adapted the following suggestions from an excellent synthesis done by Hall.[7] They are based on the career stages discussed earlier in this chapter.

1. *Exploration stage.* Since employees in this stage of career development are just beginning to discover their likes and dislikes in the work world, they have strong needs for new information and a variety of job activities. Realistic, well-integrated orientation programs are essential for employees in the exploration stage. These programs enable new employees to learn what is expected of them in their new jobs and therefore tend to eliminate that uneasy initial period in which employees sometimes grope around and learn their job responsibilities largely through trial and error.

Career planning in this stage often involves exposing employees to possibilities and choices. You can tell the new employee about the range of work assignments and job opportunities within a given department or organization, and together you and your employees can set out a plan to expose them to various job activities within the department or organization. You may decide to give either varied or special assignments to some employees or to rotate others from one job to another during the exploration stage. You may also wish to assemble detailed information on the nature of a number of jobs open to the new employee, such as that found in work performance guides, as a basis for the process of career planning.

2. *Establishment stage.* After a period of exploration, new employees choose and commit themselves to a field of work and then begin to establish themselves in their chosen line of work. This begins a new stage of determining how well they can perform. In this stage of career development, most employees begin to discover the limits of the knowledge and skill they bring to the organization. Several questions arise. What is easy or difficult for me? What do I like and dislike about this work? Have I made the right choice? How well do I really perform? Does anyone besides me recognize how well I am doing? Who is my competition for more challenging assignments and advancement? What new knowledge and skills do I have to learn to become a better performer?

During career planning interviews with employees in the establishment stage, you may need to deal with some pretty fundamental feelings that employees develop toward their work—both positive and negative. You may have to draw heavily on your counseling skills (see chapter 4) to help employees deal effectively with these feelings. Disillusionment, disappointment and self-doubt may arise. You may have to help employees address rivalry and competition. Employees may need help in recognizing that they do have gaps of knowledge and skill.

Once you and the employee have dealt effectively with these feelings, the two of you can begin making career development plans. In brief, these plans should strengthen or test an employee's potential to perform. You may select additional challenging job assignments. Additional course work in a specialty area may be needed. Employees may desire skill training to help them perform a specific job function more effectively.

3. *Advancement stage.* This stage of career development is a natural extension of the establishment stage. Once employees have settled into their field of work, they strive to progress as far as their talents and intentions will allow. Employees in the

advancement stage need a good deal of feedback about their performance and appropriate support. As they become more competent in their work, they prefer greater autonomy to be creative and innovative. Since more challenging work assignments and advancement are often accompanied by increased responsibility and demands for employees' attention and time, questions may arise regarding the relative priorities of work and family.

Designing a career development plan with employees in the advancement stage requires you to turn your attention to their talents and priorities. What special capabilities do the employees offer the organization? How far do they want to progress? What new knowledge and skill must they develop to reach their goals? When considering an employee's potential for advancement, you will have to look at the gaps between what the employee is currently doing and the performance requirements of the desired work assignment or job. Organizations are full of good technicians and professionals who were promoted into managerial jobs that they were not qualified to perform. Successful promotion requires careful study of the work performance guides for the current and desired jobs, identification of the knowledge and skills needed for the step up, and a plan on how to fill those gaps. Finally, you must resist the temptation to discourage the advancement of a particularly competent employee reporting to you. Even though you may sometimes lose your best employee to promotion, you will generally serve your needs and the needs of the organization and the employee best by encouraging each employee to advance as far as possible.

4. *Maintenance stage.* This is the stage in which employees spend the bulk of their careers, and it is the stage that presents the greatest challenge to you in the career planning interview. Employees in the maintenance stage may experience a myriad of challenges, stresses, and crises. Some employees will adjust to changes in themselves, their field of work and their organizations better than others, but all need some support if they are to continue to perform effectively and gain satisfaction in their work lives.

Career planning in the maintenance stage must be very carefully attuned to the needs of the individual employee. You will have to help each employee make plans that suit his or her own career aspirations. Some may require updating in their chosen field through individual study or through seminars and conferences. Others who wish to assume the role of mentor may need to learn not only what to do on the job, but how to coach and train younger employees. Finally, to keep them feeling challenged and to use their broad understanding of their field of work and their employer's business, still other employees in the maintenance stage may choose transfers to related jobs requiring new knowledge and skills.

5. *Retirement stage.* Career planning with employees in the retirement stage is essentially a process of gradually redirecting their focus from work to nonwork. This is the area of career planning that has received the least attention from organizations in general and potential career planners in particular. Planning for retirement should ideally begin years, rather than months, before the actual retirement date.

Employees approaching retirement face the dual challenge of withdrawing psychologically from their work and increasing their involvement and commitment in the aspects of their lives not associated with work. The need to leave a legacy is strong, especially among employees who have led very involving and successful work lives. Many employees have much to offer the organization during pre-retirement. A crucial element of career planning in the retirement stage is for you to encourage and allow retiring employees to contribute what they can. They may want to assume the role of resident expert, teacher of new employees, consultant, or reliable source of historical information, as they mold those who will take their place in the organization. With others you may simply make it clear that you do appreciate their work and that they will be missed. Whether employees approaching retirement feel passed by and useless or essential in preparing the organization for their absence depends largely on how you treat them during this crucial career stage.

PLANNING THE CAREER PLANNING INTERVIEW

Approach

As was already noted, the career planning interview is the most complex interview covered in this book, and as such it certainly requires a clear plan and structure. As always, I recommend a semistructured approach to meet the interview's objectives, but with the flexibility to allow the interviewer to respond and adjust to each individual employee.

Since the career planning interview begins with information collecting, it is necessary that as interviewers, you set out clearly the kind of information you need to collect during the interview. A similar plan is required in the information-giving portion of the interview; you will need to be familiar with the career development opportunities available in your organization that apply to the specific employee you are interviewing. Finally, since the career planning interview ends with action planning, you need to conduct the final stage of the interview with an approach of mutual goal setting.

Before the Interview

Employees should be invited and encouraged, but not required, to participate in career planning interviews. To ensure that both parties contribute to the discussion during the interview, you and your employees need to prepare thoroughly prior to the interview (See Table 5.2). Let's begin with your preparation.

Information collecting. There is a great deal you need to learn about the employee during the interview. There is, however, much you must know about the employee before you enter the interview, and this will usually necessitate some prior research into several of the following areas:

1. *Employment history.* What jobs has the employee held inside and outside your organization? What are the career rela-

Table 5.2
PLANNING THE CAREER PLANNING INTERVIEW

I. Before the Interview

    A.   Review the employee's employment history

    B.   Estimate the employee's career stage

    C.   Review the employee's performance appraisals and the steps he or she has taken to develop a career

    D.   Collect information about your company's career development opportunities

    E.   Set a meeting and clearly state its purpose

    F.   Ask the employee to:
        1. Consider his or her progress in the chosen career
        2. Think about plans for further career development

II. Format

    A.   Restate the purpose of the interview

    B.   Collect information about the employee's satisfactions and goals

    C.   Provide information about what is possible

    D.   Discuss options and set goals for career development

    E.   Propose follow-up

---

tionships among those jobs (a logical progression or not)? What functions has the employee performed and what knowledge and skill does he or she offer? What is the employee's current job and what is the work performance guide for that job?

2. *Career stage.* In which stage of career development does the employee appear to be? Is the employee still exploring? Has the employee been established for ten years? How many years is the employee from retirement? Your hunch about the employee's current career stage will help you interpret what the employee says in the interview especially concerning work satisfactions, needs, and goals.

3. *Performance appraisals.* What has been this employee's level and consistency of performance since joining your organization? A review of the employee's performance appraisal file can give you some fruitful clues to pursue in the interview. Has the employee performed very well at times, but with intermittent slumps? Has the employee consistently done just what was expected, but nothing more? You may wish to speak with the employee's previous supervisors to gain additional insight. Be careful, however, not to form firm conclusions on the basis of this review. There are many explanations of why employees perform as they do, and the most valid ones often come directly from the employees themselves. This review is not to form conclusions but, rather, to raise questions you will pursue in the interview.

4. *Employee development.* Finally, review what the employee has done to develop in his or her career. Has the employee taken every employee development course available? Has the employee requested more challenging work assignments or applied for other jobs within the company? How often has the employee been passed over for promotion? Why? This information will give you an idea of how career oriented the employee is. Some constantly seek out new developmental opportunities; others put in their eight hours and develop and experience their personal satisfaction in their nonwork lives. These clues about an employee's degree of career orientation will help you tailor the interview more toward that individual employee's needs.

Information giving. You also need to prepare your description of the career development opportunities the company offers. This information includes the types of work assignments and jobs available and the knowledge and skill required for each, as well as employee development opportunities the company provides or supports. Prior to the interview, you must arm yourself with all the information you may need to counsel employees on how they can progress in their careers. This is a very critical step. Many companies do not make employees aware of the wealth of career development opportunities they offer. As a career planning interviewer, you must have this information. But remember that you are making employees aware of what is possible. Do not make any promises or commitments unless you have the authority to deliver.

Helping the employee to prepare. Finally, you need to encourage the employee's active participation in the interview. As with other interviews with your own employees (e.g., performance appraisal), you should schedule a career planning interview ahead of time and ask the employee to come prepared. Begin the interview by stating its purpose and setting an agenda such as, "I'd like to begin by getting your views and your feelings about your current job and your work plans in the future. Then I'll fill you in on the opportunities the company has available for employee and career development. Finally, we'll work together to plot out a plan for your own career development and decide what we need to do to set the plan in action." It's important for you to set out clearly the three portions of the interview: information collecting, information giving, and mutual planning. In addition, as you schedule the meeting, ask the employee to do some thinking about:

1. His or her progress in the chosen career, and

2. Plans for further career development.

Format

Given a complex set of objectives and a semistructured approach, the career planning interview needs a format. The one outlined in Table 5.2 is recommended.

1. *Restate the purpose of the interview.* Summarizing the major objectives is a good way to remind employees of the purpose of the interview.

2. *Ask open-ended questions regarding satisfactions and goals.* Here you need to get the employee talking about how he or she feels about the job, how well he or she is performing, and the

direction of the employee's career. Be supportive during this portion of the interview and draw out themes in the employee's comments.

3. *Describe what is possible.* Now you need to add your information. Tailor your presentation to the employee's interests and needs (obviously you would not explain the company's new management trainee program to a 62-year-old employee making plans for retirement). It is important here that you not propose specific steps or give advice. Instead, offer alternatives from which employees may select what fits their needs.

4. *Discuss options and set goals for career development.* This is the portion of the interview in which employees make their choices and begin to plan. If a more challenging work assignment or specific job is desired, what knowledge and skill does the employee lack? What training is available to increase those areas of knowledge and skill? What work experience is necessary to fill the gaps? Here your focus is on *ends*, the goals the employees set, and the *means*, intervening steps and actions necessary to meet those goals.

5. *Propose follow-up.* End the career planning interview with a schedule for monitoring employee progress toward the goals. This is a crucial step if career planning is to become a genuine occurrence in a company rather than just an impressive but hollow phrase. Many companies engage in career planning, but relatively few actually plan and develop careers. Since career development is a long-term activity, it requires careful monitoring and follow-up.

CONDUCTING THE CAREER PLANNING INTERVIEW

With a set of objectives and a format forming the skeleton of the interview, let's discuss how you can proceed with conducting the career planning interview. You should rely on the standard sequence of initiate-listen-focus-probe-use in conducting the interview. In particular, this sequence will apply to the information-gathering and goal-setting stages of the interview.

Initiate. After you have restated the purpose of the interview and set the agenda, you want to enter stage 2 of the format by getting the employee talking about his or her current job and career. Begin with questions such as:

"Now that you have been with us for nearly a year as a systems analyst, what are your feelings about the job?"

or

"What aspects of your job do you find the most satisfying?"

Similarly, in stage 4, where you begin to set goals for career development, open-ended questions like the following are useful:

"Well, then, if you have no additional questions about the options open to you at this time, I'd like to turn our attention to some planning for the future. What career goals would you like to pursue?"

or

"I feel our discussion has been very fruitful so far. Let's start thinking about what happens next. What steps do you think would help you develop best in your career with us?"

Listen. Next, you must listen for points to pursue. Look for underlying themes in the employee's comments. One person's long-term interest is toward management. Another wants to remain a specialist. Still another seems uncertain and is leaning toward further exploration. Listen for any feelings, such as dissatisfaction, frustration, excitement, or impatience. These reflect needs and career stages.

Focus and Probe. As themes or issues arise in the interview that you wish to pursue in more detail, focus on them and then probe. Remember to use the nondirective techniques of reflecting a feeling or an idea and then ask a direct question to gather more information. For example:

"You sound a bit frustrated. Is there something about the work that is bothering you?"

or

"I gather that you really enjoy the challenge in that project. Would you like more challenge?"

or

"It seems to me from what you've said so far that seeing a product of your efforts on the job is pretty important to you. Is that right?"

Use. In the context of the career planning interview, this step becomes most prominent in stage 4 of the format—discussing and setting goals for development. It is important for you to avoid planning for the employee. Instead, ask what the employee wants to achieve and how he or she wants to proceed. Your role is to counsel and guide. In particular, help the employee to distinguish between ends, such as work assignments, target jobs, or long-term career goals, and means to these ends, such as home study, a training course, job rotation, or cross-training.

Your primary intention is to help employees to set a career development plan to match their work needs and career goals. As interviewer, you have the responsibility of seeing that the planning process takes place in a logical and orderly way. This occurs in stage 4 of the interviews. In the first three stages, you have established two main points:

1. What the employee wants.

2. What the company can provide or support.

   Your focus in stage 4 is on

3. How to bridge the gap between where the employee is now and where he or she wants to be.

The goals you and the employee set together will very likely fall into one or a combination of the following action plans:

1. *Change the employee*—Add knowledge, skill, or work experience through training on or off the job.

2. *Alter the job*—Change the nature of the work done by the employee by adding desired functions or eliminating undesired functions.

3. *Find a new job*—Transfer or promote an employee to meet career goals.

4. *Find a new employer*—Sometimes filling the gap between what an employee wants and what a company can provide can be done only through the employee's resignation. This may occur because of unrealistically high employee expectations or the employee's inability to develop and perform in an acceptable way. It may also occur because the company simply cannot provide the employment opportunity the employee desires.

You will have been most effective as a career planning interviewer if you and the employee leave the interview with a clear understanding of the employee's career development goal, the steps necessary to meet that goal, and a schedule for monitoring and following up.

CAREER PLANNING AND PERFORMANCE APPRAISAL

Throughout this book I have pointed out how various interviews are related to and sometimes complement one another. This is particularly true for the performance appraisal and career planning interviews. Indeed, one of the objectives of the performance appraisal interview listed in Chapter 3 is "to promote career development by discussing long-range plans for development and promotion." The systematic discussion in performance appraisal interviews of how well employees perform their work and how they can improve certainly contributes to a culture of career development in an organization and also provides raw material about the level of performance an employee is capable of achieving.

While these two types of interviews complement one another, both should be conducted regularly in organizations committed to developing and retaining their employees. There are important differences between the two types of interviews. The career planning interview builds on the performance appraisal interview and takes planning for employee development a step further. First, it provides information to employees about career development opportunities offered by the company that they otherwise might not learn about. Second, the career planning interview focuses not only on employee performance (the prime emphasis of performance appraisal interviews) but also on employee needs, motivation, and intentions. These are very important elements of the equation for matching employees with jobs. Third, career planning interviews take a longer look forward than the performance appraisal interview does in plotting the career prospects offered by the company. This longer-range planning would tend to lead to more highly integrated and career-oriented programs of employee development that would indicate to employees that remaining with one company is still a viable way to develop their careers.

OUTPLACEMENT

One possible result of a career planning interview is the realization that the employee's career development is best served by leaving the company. This may occur because the employee cannot perform to the standards necessary to advance in the company. It may also occur because the kind of work to which the employee aspires is simply unavailable in the organization. In cases where employees are terminated because of either inadequate performance or economic necessity to reduce staff, an increasing number of companies are providing outplacement service to employees.[8] This service essentially consists of career counseling and assistance in finding a new job. It is a logical extension of the career planning progress in the company. Outplacement is an excellent tool for organizations that are downsizing and choose not only to terminate employees, but also to assist their transition from one employer to another. While this service is expensive, it certainly promotes within the company a culture of commitment to employees and their career development, and I expect such outplacement service to continue in the future in major organizations.

THE PROTEAN CAREER

This chapter began with comment on how the rules governing employee behavior have changed in the recent decade. In particular, employee turnover is more acceptable, and employees have become more intent on moving to the employer who will help them most in developing their own careers. Drawing on the Greek myth of Proteus, who was able to change his shape and size at will, Hall[9] has applied the term *protean career* to this emerging set of career-related values and behavior. He defines the protean career as "a process which the person, not the organization, is managing."

Employees who aspire to the protean career (and their number is growing) want more control over their work lives. They want more freedom, more flexibility, more options, and they are willing to change jobs and employers frequently to obtain what they want. In the extreme, they are managing their own careers, in spite of their employer, rather than in collaboration with their employer. As a manager, your challenge is to enter into and contribute to the career planning process your employees are managing. If you can do so effectively, you and your organization will likely develop better employees and retain them longer. This will benefit both the employees and your organization.

Disciplinary
Interviewing

—————————————————————6

Almost all supervisors and managers will tell you that they dislike
having to discipline employees. The disciplinary interview is an
uncomfortable situation for both parties. In these interviews, bosses
often feel themselves slipping into the role of the punitive parent,
and employees feel they are being treated as children. As a result,
employees can become very defensive and argumentative, and
bosses can become exceedingly frustrated. These strong negative
emotions are certainly unpleasant for both parties and undermine
the success of the interview. Considerable skill is required to
conduct an effective disciplinary interview.

What is a disciplinary interview? It is a discussion between
an employee and his or her immediate supervisor to *correct* the
employee's failure to perform at an acceptable level. The unac-

ceptable performance can be grouped into the following two categories:

1. A violation of company policy or professional standards

2. Consistently poor performance that persists in spite of supervisory feedback, coaching, and counseling

The first category is usually triggered by a specific incident, such as unexcused absenteeism or tardiness, violation of a safety procedure, or a salesperson's unauthorized price reduction to meet a sales quota. The second category includes sub-standard job performance, which the manager has already discussed with the employee in day-to-day feedback, performance appraisals, or counseling, but which the employee has not improved.

Progressive Discipline

Beginning in the 1960s, federal and state statutes and judicial decisions have severely limited the right of employers to terminate an employee at will.[1] To ensure that employees are treated consistently and fairly, and to avoid lawsuits for "wrongful discharge," many employers have established formal discipline policies to guide supervisors and managers in dealing with unacceptable employee performance.[2] Such policies are included in union contracts in organized settings, but they are also common in organizations with no unionized employees.

Legal, effective disciplinary policies are *progressive* and *corrective*.[3] They consist of a series of disciplinary actions, each of which is intended to correct the unacceptable performance, not to punish the employee (see Table 6.1). As managers, you can implement progressive discipline successfully by following the "hot stove" principle. Anyone who touches a hot stove, regardless of race, color, sex, age, etc, receives an *immediate, consistent, impartial* response. You should respond with the appropriate disciplinary action as soon as possible after the employee's unacceptable performance, with every employee reporting to you, every time

Table 6.1
DISCIPLINE POLICY[4]

Policy Statement

It is the explicit intention of the Company for discipline to be administered fairly, on a timely basis, and without prejudice. Within reasonable limits, the principles of good conduct and businesslike behavior will apply and be maintained.

Possible Disciplinary Actions

Verbal Reprimand

A verbal reprimand is used for minor violations. Circumstances which may warrant this type of discipline include, but are not limited to, the beginning of an absence/tardiness problem or minor inattention to good work practices. One, but no more than two, verbal reprimands for the same violation should lead to a written reprimand.

Written Reprimand

A written reprimand is used in cases where verbal reprimand has not proven corrective. It is also appropriate for first violations of clearly stated rules and regulations and generally when a violation is considered serious enough to place a written record in the employee's personnel file.

Layoff

Layoff results in the employee being relieved of his/her duties and, if possible, being asked to leave the premises immediately. This step is taken for violations of a serious nature, such as, but not limited to, the following:

1. When written reprimand has not proven corrective.
2. Insubordination.
3. Willful destruction of Company property.
4. Theft of Company or other employee's property.
5. Being under the influence of intoxicants or drugs on Company premises.
6. Assault, battery, or harassment of a fellow employee.
7. Gross misconduct on Company premises.
8. Failure to follow published safety directives or other Company policy.
9. Breach of Company's equal employment policy regarding non-discrimination because of a person's race, color, religion, national origin, or sex.

Any violations of numbers 2 through 8 may lead directly to discharge, depending on the circumstances involved.

The laid off employee should be asked to leave the premises immediately, if possible. He/she will be instructed to remain off duty until contacted.

Discharge

Discharge of an employee may result from, but is not limited to the following:

1. Repeated violations where layoff and reprimand have not been corrective.
2. Violations of numbers 2 through 9 listed under "Layoff."

(continued on next page)

Table 6.1 (cont.)

3. Conviction of a major crime.
4. Deliberate misrepresentation in order to obtain employment.
5. Defrauding or attempting to defraud the Company.
6. Violations which have always resulted in discharge.

The procedure for discharge is essentially the same as for layoff. The employee is relieved of duties and asked to leave the premises immediately, if possible. The employee should understand that he/she is being considered for discharge and will be advised as soon as final disposition is made.

Documentation of Disciplinary Action

The form, Supervisor's Personnel Report, is used to record a written reprimand, layoff, or discharge. The employee should sign all copies and be given one copy in the event of written reprimand or layoff. Should the employee refuse to sign the report, note the reason for the refusal on the last line. The forms should be completed in a clear and concise manner, and the "Action Taken" section must summarize what is being done for the current violation and what the consequences of future violations will be.

---

it occurs. Corrective action may vary, as we shall discuss later in the chapter, but the initial disciplinary action should not.

Unfortunately, many supervisors avoid confronting employees who have performed unacceptably, either by violating a company policy or professional standard, or by consistently performing poorly. These supervisors allow some employees to "bend the rules" while enforcing policies with others, and therefore invite accusations of favoritism or prejudice, and even lawsuits. Others give acceptable performance appraisals to poor performers year after year, and then when they finally decide to confront the problem, the employee and his or her lawyer can produce a large file that documents the employee's long record of acceptable performance. As managers, you may not like the "hot stove" principle, but it provides the only way for you to be fair to all employees and to truly take corrective action.

The disciplinary interview takes place in the first step of progressive discipline, usually called a verbal warning or verbal reprimand. Supervisors and managers can solve the vast majority of disciplinary problems at this step. Failure to correct the employee's unacceptable performance with a disciplinary interview, however, leads to increasingly more legalistic steps that may eventually result in discharge. Although many organizations instruct managers in their disciplinary policies, far too few actually provide hands-on training in how to carry out the verbal warning successfully by conducting an effective disciplinary interview. That is the purpose of this chapter.

WHY DISCIPLINARY INTERVIEWS ARE NECESSARY

A crucial first step to changing employee performance is to understand the cause of the performance. There are, of course, a large number of reasons that employees fail to perform up to the standards of their supervisors or according to company policy, but they can be grouped into a manageable number of categories.

1. *Employee is not capable.* There are many instances in which an employee's lack of performance can be traced simply to his or her inability to perform the job acceptably well. The employee does not have the necessary knowledge and skill to perform up to standard. If the disciplinary interview is conducted effectively and the cause is identified, these cases should not go beyond the initial verbal warning. Corrective action may involve training, redefinition of the current job, or even placement in another job.

2. *Employee doesn't know the rules.* A major and distressingly common cause of poor employee performance is lack of clear job definition and feedback from the supervisor. A remarkably large number of employees simply do not know what is expected of them on the job. In these cases a major portion of the responsibility for unacceptable performance rests squarely on the shoulders of the immediate supervisor. The source of the problem may be a lack of job descriptions, unclear instructions being given by the supervisor, an inadequate performance appraisal system, an absence of company operating procedures for various jobs, or supervisors

who do not give feedback to their employees. Corrective action in these instances is two-fold. First, jobs must be structured and defined in such a way that employees know what is expected of them. Second, supervisors and employees must discuss employee performance periodically and take appropriate action to improve each employee's work.

3. *Employee resists performing well.* This is the most common cause of unacceptable performance and the most difficult to correct. Employees know what is expected of them and are capable of performing up to standard, but their performance is inconsistent and unpredictable. In this category we find the so-called "problem employee" with a "poor attitude." These employees appear to lack the degree of commitment required to do their best at work. The root of their unacceptable performance is either the low priority that they attach to their work lives or a strong dissatisfaction with a major element of their current work situation—the work itself, salary, co-workers, the company, the boss, or opportunities for promotion. Corrective action with these employees requires that the source of their dissatisfaction be uncovered and addressed.

OBJECTIVES

As managers and supervisors, it is essential that you have a clear idea of what you intend to achieve in the disciplinary interview. Knowing your objectives is particularly important in this interview because it is triggered by some sort of problem and almost invariably leads to emotional reactions from both parties. Unless you have clearly in mind what you want to achieve, you can easily be sidetracked or even lose control of the interview.

There are three basic objectives in the disciplinary interview. They are:

1. *Define the situation*—Clearly describe the incident of unacceptable performance that has triggered the interview.

2. *Pinpoint the responsibility for the unacceptable performance*—
Examine the causes of the unacceptable performance from
both the supervisor's and the employee's point of view.

3. *Plan the corrective action*—Set out a specific plan of action
to reduce or eliminate the unacceptable performance.

In the case of the disciplinary interview, these objectives
also represent conditions for success. Each of the three is extremely
crucial and furthermore, each must be met effectively before those
following it can even be addressed. In short, you must achieve
each objective well, and you must address all three of them in
the sequence given.

Define the situation. In the first objective, you and your
employee must clearly establish the reason for the interview, namely,
the unacceptable performance. It is necessary that both parties
give their perceptions of the incident that triggered the interview.
Special attention should be given to:

1. Exactly what the employee did that is viewed as unacceptable.

2. The severity of the employee's unacceptable performance.

3. What the employee was supposed to have done.

4. The circumstances surrounding the incident.

Here the policies and standards of the organization and the supervisor
come into play. As the interviewer, you must consider how much
human error is inevitable and how severe or chronic the unacceptable
performance actually is. As Table 6.1 indicates, some types of
unacceptable performance result in immediate layoff or even discharge. In these instances the supervisor does not even give a
verbal warning and therefore conducts no disciplinary interview.

Pinpoint the responsibility for the unacceptable performance.
The second objective is to examine the factors and circumstances
that contributed to the unacceptable performance. Which of the three
general reasons why employees fail to perform (employee is not
capable, employee doesn't know the rules, or employee resists per-

forming well) seems to apply in this particular case? The views of both the supervisor and the employee must be brought out. A reminder: It is crucial that you keep your mind open to the possibility that you contributed to the problem either by not clearly defining the employee's job and your performance standards or by not giving the employee clear and consistent feedback.

Plan the corrective action. Finally, in the third objective, you and your employee must turn toward the future. After you have identified the unacceptable performance and its cause, you must take whatever steps are necessary to reduce or eliminate the unacceptable performance. The disciplinary process can be *corrective* if the interview ends only after you and the employee have addressed this objective fully. The interview should end with a specific plan of action endorsed by you and, as often as possible, also by your employee.

PLANNING THE DISCIPLINARY INTERVIEW

Approach

The disciplinary interview should be approached with a clear plan and a well-defined format. The result will be a semistructured interview. The hallmark of the disciplinary interview is direct and clear communication and mild confrontation. By this I mean that you must be direct and clear in identifying the unacceptable performance that prompted the verbal warning. Beating around the bush or being evasive will only confuse the employee. In addition, you must be prepared to confront the employee by pointing out inconsistencies in what he or she has said and done.

Before the Interview

In planning a disciplinary interview, you must collect a good deal of information that you can use during the interview. You must be prepared with facts that are properly documented. You

Table 6.2
PLANNING THE DISCIPLINARY INTERVIEW

I. **Before the Interview**

    A.   Review and properly document the unacceptable performance

    B.   Review performance appraisals for clues

    C.   Check your broad understanding of the employee

II. **Format**

    A.   Set the ground rules

    B.   Discuss the unacceptable performance

    C.   Discuss reasons for the unacceptable performance

    D.   Make plans for change

---

must also do some research to try to understand the particular employee whom you are disciplining. This research will provide the background against which you can interpret what the employee did that triggered the interview and what he or she says during the interview. There are three major steps in this planning process, outlined in Table 6.2.

Step 1: Review and properly document employee performance. This is a crucial first step. As the interviewer, you must collect all the facts concerning what the employee did or failed to do, and what the results of the unacceptable performance were. Be sure to follow your organization's progressive discipline policy by properly documenting the events that led to the verbal warning. In addition, remember the "hot stove" principle. When you become aware of the unacceptable performance, you must respond as soon as possible and consistently, regardless of who the employee is.

It is also essential that you examine the circumstances under which the unacceptable performance occurred. How have you or the organization contributed to this employee's behavior? Were you clear in your instructions to the employee? Are the job and this employee's specific responsibilities clearly defined? Is company policy clear on this violation? Have you, through inadequate feedback, allowed the employee to get away with this before? Be honest with yourself as you seek to uncover any way in which you must share responsibility for your employee's action.

Step 2: Review performance appraisals for clues. The next step is to review the employee's past performance either through formal performance appraisal files or your own recollection. Has the employee's performance been consistent or inconsistent? How well has this individual typically done in the past? Is this an unusual slump in an otherwise consistent and excellent record, or is this one more incident in a long stream of unacceptable performance?

A particularly fruitful portion of the performance appraisal file is plans for employee development. Review these for several years to see if they have been acted on either by the employee or by the organization. Has the employee been turned down for a transfer or special training three years in succession? Did the employee perform poorly in a rotation program just before his or her recent promotion? Be on the lookout either for signs of the employee's inability to do the job or signs of frustration and anger in his or her work life. Why has this employee performed poorly?

Step 3: Check your broad understanding of the employee. Finally, reflect on your overall understanding of your employee. Why would the employee do such a thing? This behavior is unusual; what's changed? Although we may work with people 40 hours week, we really know little about them. Think back. What has happened on or off the job to frustrate, upset, or disillusion the employee? Form your hunches now and be prepared to examine them in the interview. It is essential that you respond to the unacceptable performance with a verbal warning regardless of the employee involved. What you learn about that employee in steps 2 and 3, however, will help you understand the reasons for the performance and will also help you decide on the appropriate corrective action.

Format

As with other interviews covered in this book, I recommend a semistructured approach to the disciplinary interview. There are three objectives to be met and many questions to be answered in this interview, but the approach must be flexible enough to enable you to adjust the interview to the individual employee. There is, however, a basic format, outlined in Table 6.2, that forms the skeleton of the disciplinary interview.

1. *Set the ground rules.* As the supervisor, it is important that you clearly state the purpose of your meeting with the employee. Begin by stating that you are very concerned about the unacceptable performance and that you are initiating the organization's progressive discipline procedure with a verbal warning. Clarify your intention in the interview by stating that you would like to discuss the unacceptable performance in more detail and come up with a plan to prevent its recurrence. Emphasize also that you are very interested in the employee's point of view.

2. *Discuss the unacceptable performance.* It is preferable to begin by briefly summarizing the unacceptable performance and then asking for the employee's perception of exactly what happened and why. In this section of the interview, it is necessary that you draw out details concerning what the employee did or failed to do, the circumstances surrounding the behavior, and the results of the behavior. After the employee has expressed his or her view, you present your perception of the unacceptable performance. The main purpose in this section of the interview is to describe what happened, from the point of view of both the employee and the supervisor.

3. *Examine the causes of the unacceptable performance.* Here you are examining the factors that contributed to the employee's unacceptable performance. The types of questions you ask will depend on the type of unacceptable performance. If the employee has violated company policy or professional standards, ask *what occurred*, and *why* the employee behaved as he or she did. If

the employee has continued to perform poorly in spite of your feedback and counseling, your probing should be more detailed. Use the same types of probes that were discussed in the chapter on performance appraisal interviewing. Ask *how* the employee approaches that part of the job on which performance is poor, *why* the employee uses that approach, *how well* the approach works, and what the employee thinks he or she could *do differently* to improve the performance. These types of questions (illustrated in the next section) will help you investigate each of the three reasons why employees fail to perform (employee not capable, employee doesn't know the rules, and employee resists performing well) to insure a thorough understanding of all potential causes.

4. *Make plans for change.* After a thorough diagnosis of the reasons for the unacceptable performance, the final step is to plan corrective action. Before the interview is closed, you and your employee should have a set of specific goals or assignments to be pursued by the employee with appropriate support from you or others in the organization.

CONDUCTING THE DISCIPLINARY INTERVIEW

The format, based on a set of objectives, forms the skeleton of the disciplinary interview. As with all other interviews in this book, the disciplinary interview comes to life through the skills and techniques you use in conducting it. The skill of conducting the interview is particularly important in the disciplinary interview. You must be direct, clear, and firm. You must move through the entire interview format to cover all three objectives. You must deal on the spot with a variety of reactions from your employees; they may become very emotional, distort information, or even lie.

Your main challenges in conducting the disciplinary interview are to draw out and examine what your employee has to say, to use mild confrontation to separate fact from fiction, and to make constructive use of the information you gain. To meet these challenges, you should rely on the familiar sequence of initiate-listen-focus-probe-use. More specifically, in the second and third sections of the format (discuss the unacceptable performance and examine the reasons for the unacceptable performance), you will use the first four steps in the sequence to gather information. In the fourth section of the interview (make plans for change), you and the employee will focus on the last step in the sequence.

Initiate. Begin the discussion by expressing your concern with the unacceptable performance and use open-ended questions to encourage the employee to talk about the performance. Let's consider an example of each type of unacceptable performance. In the first, a bright, competent clerical employee has begun to extend her breaks and lunch hours beyond the allowed time off. In addition, her performance has dropped in the past two months. Today, she returned from lunch one hour late and was unavailable to take on an important assignment. Her supervisor has called her in for a verbal warning for violating the time-off policy.

> "Sally, I noticed that you returned from lunch an hour late today. I had an important assignment for you and couldn't find you anywhere. As you know, we have already discussed your tardiness and drop in performance during the past two months on three occasions. I am very concerned about this pattern of behavior and have decided to initiate our disciplinary process with a verbal warning. Let's begin with lunch today. What happened?"

The second example deals with a supervisor with 35 years in the same industry. He started out on the assembly line and worked his way up to a supervisory position 20 years ago. He supervises a group of engineers very closely, delegates only routine assignments, and keeps the most challenging work to himself. He has a long history of low morale and high turnover in his area; employees complain that he treats them like children. His manager has tried unsuccessfully to change this supervisory style in the past two performance appraisal interviews. Two resignations and a request for transfer have convinced the manager that this supervisory style cannot continue. She has decided to begin progressive discipline with a verbal warning.

> "As you know, Carl, two of your engineering staff quit and a third asked to be transferred this past week. We have discussed the level of morale and turnover in your group in our last two performance appraisals, but the problem has only worsened. I am very concerned about the turnover in your department and have decided to take disciplinary action with you with a verbal warning. What in your view contributed to the loss of these three employees last week?"

Listen. As the employee responds to your open-ended questions, you should listen very carefully for points you wish to pursue. During Sally's description of what happened during her lunch hour, listen for points that need elaboration or clarification. While Carl complains that young employees expect too much too soon today, listen for contradictions or points of contention. As a general rule, listen for questions that arise and must be examined further.

Remember that during this portion of the interview, your task is to collect information from the employee. Do so, silently. You must resist the temptation to interrupt and voice your opinion. At this point, you need to keep the channels of communication wide open to learn as much as possible. If you hear something that you disagree with or find confusing, store it in your memory for additional examination later. If you feel you are being lied to, avoid confronting the employee immediately. Give the employee a few minutes to make his or her presentation as a whole and then move in with your additional questioning. In short, while you are listening, suspend judgment and avoid interrupting or delivering a lecture.

Focus and Probe. As always, this is where you do your real work in the interview. Focusing on specific points and probing them in more detail is particularly important in the disciplinary interview. You and your employee are at odds with one another. You will hear things that you disagree with or strongly oppose. It is your main task in the disciplinary interview to get these points out on the table and to deal with them in a direct and clear manner.

You will move through the initiate-listen-focus-probe sequence first as you examine the employee's perception of the unacceptable performance and then again as the employee discusses it in more detail. In each case, when you begin to focus and probe, start with issues that are not highly contentious. Begin with issues that are least likely to make the employee feel defensive. For example:

> "You mentioned, Camille, that by the time you realized that you had forgotten to notify the committee members of the meeting, it was too late to do anything. When did you realize that you had forgotten to notify them?"

> or

> "And you said that you felt the situation didn't warrant standard safety precautions. What factors did you consider in making that judgment?"

In these illustrations you are seeking more information so that you can understand more clearly what the employee did and why. It is crucial that you probe these areas in as neutral a fashion as possible, so the employee does not feel attacked and as a result, say little in response.

In our earlier example of Carl's supervisory style causing low morale and turnover among his staff, the manager needed to use several probing questions to examine potential causes of the recent turnover. Let's pick up their discussion early in the interview.

> INTERVIEWER: "So, Carl, you think the primary reason for the resignations and transfer is that young engineers are so impatient today. It that it?"

EMPLOYEE: "You bet. They think they know everything and want me to assign them the most difficult projects too early. That's not the way I came up in this company."

INTERVIEWER: "I see. How do you decide which projects to assign your people?"

EMPLOYEE: "I like to bring them along slowly. I start them out with the routine stuff, and I check their work very carefully."

INTERVIEWER: "Why do you do it that way, Carl?"

EMPLOYEE: "That's the way it was done with me! Anyway, I don't trust the newcomers to do the work right. If their work is not up to standard, I get the blame."

INTERVIEWER: "How's that style of supervision working out for you?"

EMPLOYEE: "Great. We have the lowest error rate in the entire department!"

INTERVIEWER: "That's true, Carl, and I really appreciate your attention to company standards. But I am concerned about the amount of overtime you're working. How many hours have you been averaging in the past six months?"

EMPLOYEE: "I've been putting in 60-hour weeks. Maybe I could cut back if these kids wouldn't quit so often."

INTERVIEWER: "As we discussed in your last two performance appraisals, Carl, I think your supervisory style is contributing to your turnover. Is there any way you think you can keep your error rate low and also bring down this turnover?"

As the discussion continues, Carl begins to realize that he is supervising his current staff too closely. Plans are made to give Carl some training and coaching in delegation.

As you continue to focus and probe, you will need to work up to more contentious issues. These issues can take a variety of forms. You may find contradictions between what employees say and what they do. You may hear distortions of facts or outright lies. You may hear complaining and whining rather than valid reasons for inadequate performance. In these kinds of cases, you will have to confront employees with the discrepancy between what they say in the interview and the facts as you perceive them. Remember, though, your information may be wrong. Therefore, I advise you to confront the employee with the discrepancy and ask for an explanation. Consider the following two examples:

A clerical employee in a branch bank has taken a parking pass from her manager's desk to cover her parking fee in a nearby lot. Bank policy states that these parking passes are available to customers only. The manager began the next day's work with a disciplinary interview. After hearing the employee's explanation of what occurred and why, the manager confronts the employee in the following way:

> INTERVIEWER: "You said earlier that you used the parking pass only because a loan officer gave you permission to use it. That simply doesn't fit with what I've learned about this incident. I saw you talking with three deposit clerks at the counter and when I talked to them later, each said you asked for a parking pass for your own use. Furthermore, I've checked my supply of passes, and one is missing. How do you explain the discrepancy between your explanation and what I have just said?"

The performance of a young person who has been in an entry-level job for six months has fallen off dramatically in the past two months. After commenting on the drop in performance on several occasions, and conducting a counseling interview with the employee, the manager has called the employee in for a verbal warning.

> INTERVIEWER: "So your main explanation for your drop in performance is that you are disappointed with the nature of the work. You feel that you have not been challenged enough on the job. Does that pretty well summarize what you said earlier?"

EMPLOYEE: "Yes, I really feel frankly that I was promised a lot more than the company has delivered so far."

INTERVIEWER: "To be equally frank with you, I'm having trouble accepting your explanation. On three specific occasions in the last six weeks I've asked you to take on a special assignment and you've refused. Furthermore, in our last monthly meeting of all the trainees, I asked for volunteers to transfer to another section to learn additional functions of the department and you were the only one who didn't raise his hand. In view of this, how do you expect me to believe that you really want more challenging work?"

In each of these illustrations, the interviewer focused on a point of contention and then confronted the employee with an apparent discrepancy. This is essential to bring these contentious issues to a head. You must address them directly.

Use. The final step in the sequence for conducting the disciplinary interview is to make use of the information you have collected up to this point in the interview to meet the third objective: planning the corrective action. Since this interview may be the final step that you take to correct unacceptable performance, it is essential that you and the employee leave the interview with a clear understanding of the situation and a clear plan. Let's return to the three groups of reasons for unacceptable performance and consider how you can use the information you gain in the interview.

1. *Employee is not capable.* If you are interviewing an employee who appears to lack the knowledge and skill to perform all aspects of the job successfully, you must either alter the employee's potential to do the job or move him or her to another job. In these cases, it is essential that you focus and probe to diagnose in detail what aspects of the job the employee is failing to perform and what he or she is lacking. On the basis of this analysis, your plans for change may involve training, a new configuration of job responsibilities, transfer to another job, or even termination.

Before you end the interview you must make certain that the employee understands that he or she is failing to meet your performance standards and why, and what corrective action is appropriate.

2. *Employee doesn't know the rules.* If you learn during the focus and probe stage of the interview that the employee truly did not know what was expected of him or her, clarify what the employee did know and how the employee learned it. Then before ending the interview, make your performance standards and company policies absolutely clear. In addition, be sure to check the employee's understanding of what you have said.

3. *Employee resists performing well.* These are particularly tough cases. The employee you are dealing with may be quite capable of performing well but does not. As mentioned earlier, while you focus and probe, you will need to mildly confront this type of employee. It is important, however, not to slip into the role of the punitive parent. Instead, you must use what you have learned about the employee's reasons for failing to perform or violating a policy by shifting the responsibility for change to the employee. Ask the employee what steps he or she will take to improve. Ask the employee to give you the reasons that he or she should not be terminated for such actions. A useful tactic[5] is to suspend the employee for a day with pay and ask him or her to return with a decision to resign or remain with the company and if the employee chooses to remain, a plan for improving performance.

Don'ts of Disciplinary Interviewing

Because the disciplinary interview can be a highly emotional situation that can erupt into a major confrontation, it is essential that you avoid falling into traps that will cause the employee to become defensive and argumentative. Here are some pointers to help you avoid the role of punitive parent.

1. *Don't criticize the employee personally.* Like personal feedback in the performance appraisal interview, making vague, general statements about the employee in the disciplinary interview will get you nothing but trouble. Don't comment on the employee's attitude, don't tell her she's unmotivated, or don't tell him that he doesn't seem to care. These are highly subjective conclusions that make employees feel labeled and personally attacked. Since they are opinions, they are also open to interpretation and debate.

2. *Don't interrupt or argue.* While collecting information from the employee, you must avoid interrupting and stating your own views as soon as you hear something you disagree with. Doing so will either result in a shouting match or make the employee say less than you need to hear.

3. *Don't do all the work.* Avoid taking a very active role in the interview. For example, do not make all the assessments of why the employee performs as he or she does, and do not make all the proposals for change.

4. *Don't issue ultimatums.* An ultimatum offers just one option, and it will make the employee feel powerless and trapped. Furthermore, issuing an ultimatum places a lot of responsibility on you. You must consider all the options and select the one that is most appropriate. Then you must order the employee to follow that selected option "or else." Finally, if the employee follows your ultimatum and still fails, the employee may blame you for ordering him or her to take the wrong proposal.

Do's of Disciplinary Interviewing

You must be direct and clear to ensure that the employee understands what you are saying. The following guides will help you to conduct the interview in a firm, straightforward, constructive manner.

1. *Do give specific behavioral feedback.* Instead of stating general conclusions, describe clearly and concisely what you have seen the employee doing. Then ask the employee to explain why. This keeps the focus of the interview on facts, rather than opinions,

and puts some responsibility on the employee to consider the causes of his or her own performance.

2. *Do listen.* Listen carefully when the employee is talking. Make a mental note of information you question, but wait until later to address it.

3. *Do draw out the employee's ideas.* You need to work very hard with open-ended questions and specific probes to get the employee's perceptions of the reasons for his or her performance and what the employee can do to change. Employees must be given a complete and fair hearing especially in cases where the verbal warning may be followed by more severe disciplinary actions. Moreover, their explanations and ideas may be valid.

4. *Do offer choices.* Adults must be given the freedom to accept responsibility for their own work lives by generating alternatives and making choices. Give employees the opportunity of analyzing their own predicaments and proposing their own plans for change. Suspension with pay is a good illustration of this principle. You still retain the option of rejecting a proposal that you consider inappropriate. Furthermore, if you approve an employee's proposal for corrective action that he or she follows without success, you can hold the employee responsible for the failure.

5. *Do be clear and direct.* Finally, throughout the disciplinary interview, you must be clear and straightforward. Some supervisors, when faced with a potentially unpleasant disciplinary interview, talk around the problem and hope the employee will catch on and take corrective action. This only confuses and irritates the employee. When you have something to say in this interview, you must say it clearly and without hesitation.

REDUCING THE NEED FOR DISCIPLINARY INTERVIEWS

Disciplinary interviews represent a last resort to ensuring that employee performance meets supervisory standards and company policy. While some measure of unacceptable performance is inevitable, its occurrence can certainly be reduced. Several steps can be taken to minimize unacceptable performance and therefore reduce the need for conducting disciplinary interviews. Let's consider some of them.

Make the rules clear. Far more often than necessary, employees simply do not know what is expected of them on the job. Job descriptions can be found, but they are often too general and out of date. Performance appraisal forms exist, but new employees do not see one until the boss has filled it out three or six months after they have started work. Company policies may be described in detail in a lengthy manual, but new employees may not read them thoroughly.

As a supervisor or manager, you must take a more active role in setting out the job responsibilities, performance standards, and company policies and rules which govern your employees' performance. Now I'm not suggesting that you spoon-feed your employees. Certainly, you can and should expect them to take some initiative and seek out this kind of information. But you do need to follow up and test their understanding of your expectations. Don't assume too much. My rule of thumb is, when in doubt, be explicit. Spell it out. Your employees will perform better and you'll be a more effective supervisor if you give them too much information rather than too little. Further, you eliminate the naive excuses supervisors sometimes hear from employees in the disciplinary interview, such as, "I didn't know I was (or wasn't) supposed to do that."

Give clear and consistent feedback. As a supervisor or manager, you must direct, control, and evaluate the performance of the employees reporting to you. If in your day-to-day contact with employees you give them feedback on their performance, you can reduce the frequency of unacceptable performance and therefore the need for more formal disciplinary interviews. Your employees need specific behavioral feedback when they perform well or poorly. Immediate and clear feedback is especially important when employees have violated an important policy or performed very poorly. Deal with the incident on the spot with feedback and some coaching to help prevent similar incidents. Above all, don't shy away from telling employees when they have done something that is unacceptable.

Make full use of other interviews. Finally, the need for a disciplinary interview can sometimes indicate that in other interviews you may have failed to meet your objectives fully. It's your job as a supervisor or manager to know your employees. In addition to your daily or weekly contact with them, some of the interviews covered in this book provide a vehicle for you to learn about your employees. You may be able to detect and deal with potential causes of unacceptable performance in performance appraisal or career planning interviews before that performance becomes so frequent or severe that it requires disciplinary action. Counseling interviews can also help you diagnose problems such as employee dissatisfaction or inadequate training before they lead to major incidents of unacceptable performance. Finally, effective selection interviews can prevent your organization from adding a chronically poor performer or a disciplinary problem. In short, proper use of these other interviews will reduce the number of times you have to make use of your last resort, the disciplinary interview.

Endnotes

Chapter 1

1. For example, see J. G. Allen, *The Complete Q & A Job Interview Book* (New York: Wiley, 1988);

   R. H. Beatty, *The Five Minute Interview* (New York: Wiley, 1986);

   R. Half, *How to Get a Better Job in This Crazy World* (New York: Crown Publishers, 1990);

   E. Rushlow, *Get a Better Job!* (Princeton, NJ: Peterson's Guides, 1990); and

   M. J. Yate, *Knock 'Em Dead with Great Answers to Tough Questions* (Boston: Bob Adams, Inc, 1991).

Chapter 2

1. J. Solomon, "The New Job Interview: Show Thyself," *Wall Street Journal*, December 4, 1989, B1, B6.

2. S. L. Rynes, "The Employment Interview as a Recruitment Device," In R. W. Eder & G. R. Ferris (Eds), *The Employment Interview: Theory, Research, and Practice* (Newbury Park, CA: SAGE Publications, 1989), 127–141; and

   J. P. Wanous, *Organizational Entry: Recruitment, Selection, Orientation, and Socialization of Newcomers.* 2nd ed. (Reading, MA: Addison-Wesley, 1992).

3. M. Gibb-Clark, "Breaking Hiring Promises Proves Costly for Firms, Case Reveals," *Globe and Mail*, October 6, 1988, B3.

4. W. D. Scott, "The Scientific Selection of Salesmen," *Advertising and Selling*, 25 (1915), 5, 6, 94–96.

5. R. Wagner, "The Employment Interview: A Critical Summary," *Personnel Psychology*, 2 (Spring 1949), 17–46;

   E. C. Mayfield, "The Selection Interview: A Re-evaluation of Published Research," *Personnel Psychology*, 17 (Autumn 1964), 239–260;

   N. Schmitt, "Socal and Situational Determinants of Interview Decisions: Implications for the Employment Interview," *Personnel Psychology*, 29 (Spring 1976), 79–101; and

   W. H. Wiesner & S. F. Cronshaw, "The Moderating Impact of Interview Format and Degree of Structure on Interview Validity," *The Journal of Occupational Psychology*, 61 (1988), 275–290.

6. R. W. Eder & G. R. Ferris (Eds), *The Employment Interview: Theory, Research, and Practice*.

7. J. G. Goodale, "Effective Employment Interviewing," In R. W. Eder & G. R. Ferris (Eds), *The Employment Interview: Theory, Research, and Practice*, 307–323.

8. R. M. Guion, *Personnel Testing* (New York: McGraw-Hill, 1965); and

   J. G. Goodale, "Effective Employment Interviewing."

9. E. C. Mayfield, "The Selection Interview: A Re-evaluation of Published Research;" and

   P. M. Rowe, "Unfavorable Information and Interview Decisions," In R. W. Eder & G. R. Ferris (Eds), *The Employment Interview: Theory, Research, and Practice*, 77–89.

10. M. D. Hakel, T. D. Hollman, & M. D. Dunnette, "Accuracy of Interviewers, Certified Public Accountants, and Students in Identifying the Interests of Accountants." *Journal of Applied Psychology*, 54 (1970), 115–119.

11. E. C. Webster, *The Employment Interview: A Social Judgment Process* (Schomberg, Ontario: S.I.P., 1982); and

    P. M. Rowe, "Unfavorable Information and Interview Decisions."

12. R. E. Carlson, P. W. Thayer, E. C. Mayfield, & D. A. Peterson, "Improvements in the Selection Interview," *Personnel Journal*, 50 (April 1971), 268–275, 317.

13. For additional information, see K. McCulloch, *Selecting Employees Safely under the Law* (Englewood Cliffs, N.J.: Prentice Hall, 1981); and

    J. Ledvinka and V. G. Scarpello, *Federal Regulation of Personnel and Human Resource Management* (Boston: PWS-Kent Publishing, 1990).

14. J. E. Campion & R. D. Arvey, "Unfair Discrimination in the Employment Interview," in R. W. Eder and G. R. Ferris (Eds), *The Employment Interview: Theory, Research, and Practice*, 61–73.

15. J. E. Campion & R. D. Arvey, "Unfair Discrimination in the Employment Interview."

16. S. L. Rynes, "The Employment Interview as a Recruitment Device"; and

    J. P. Wanous, "Effects of a Realistic Job Preview on Job Acceptance, Job Attitudes, and Job Survival," *Journal of Applied Psychology*, 53 (1973), 327–332.

17. For detailed instructions on validating selection devices, see "Uniform Guidelines on Employee Selection Procedures," *Federal Register*, Part IV, August 25, 1978.

Chapter 3

1. H. H. Meyer, "A Solution to the Performance Appraisal Feedback Enigma," *The Executive*, 5 (February 1991), 68–76.

2. C. O. Longnecker, "Truth or Consequences: Politics and Performance Appraisals," *Business Horizons*, November-December 1989, 76–82;

   M. A. Verespej, "Performance Reviews Get Mixed Reviews," *Industry Week*, August 20, 1990, 49–54;

   R. Zemke, "Do Performance Appraisals Change Performance?" *Training*, 28 (May 1991), 34–39;

R. L. Taylor & R. A. Zawacki, "Trends in Performance Appraisal: Guidelines for Managers," *Personnel Administrator*, March 1984, 71–80; and

R. J. Burke, "Why Performance Appraisal Systems Fail," *Personnel Administration*, 34 (May-June 1972), 32–40.

3. H. H. Meyer, E. Kay, & J. P. R. French, Jr., "Split Roles in Performance Appraisal," *Harvard Business Review*, 43 (January-February 1965), 123–129.

4. H. H. Meyer, "A Solution to the Performance Appraisal Feedback Enigma";

D. J. Campbell & C. Lee, "Self-appraisal in Performance Evaluation: Development Versus Evaluation," *Academy of Management Review*, 13 (April 1988), 302–324;

L. D. Foxman & W. L. Polsky, "Performance Appraisals Are Not Salary Reviews," *Personnel Journal*, October 1988, 30–32; and

J. L. Hall, B. Z. Posner, & J. W. Harder, "Performance Appraisal Systems: Matching Practice with Theory," *Group and Organization Studies*, 14 (March 1989), 51–69.

5. E. E. Lawler, III, A. M. Mohrman, Jr., & S. M. Resnick, "Performance Appraisal Revisited," *Organizational Dynamics*, 13 (Summer 1984), 20–35.

6. D. T. Hall, & J. G. Goodale, *Human Resource Management: Strategy, Design, and Implementation* (Glenview, IL: Scott-Foresman, 1986). See Chapter 15.

7. "Uniform Guidelines on Employee Selection Procedures," *Federal Register*, Part IV, August 25, 1978.

8. G. L. Lubben, D. E. Thompson, & C. R. Klasson, "Performance Appraisal: The Legal Implications of Title VII." *Personnel*, 57 (May-June 1980), 11–21;

H. J. Bernardin & R. W. Beatty, *Performance Appraisal: Assessing Human Behavior at Work.* (Boston: Kent Publishing, 1984), 42–61; and

R. W. Goddard, "Is Your Appraisal System Headed for Court?" *Personnel Journal*, January 1989, 114–118.

9. E. J. Pollock, "Better Confrontation than Discrimination?" *Wall Street Journal*, May 14, 1991, B1.

10. P. C. Smith & L. M. Kendall, "Retranslation of Expectations: An Approach to the Construction of Unambiguous Anchors for Rating Scales," *Journal of Applied Psychology*, 47 (1963), 249–255; and

    G. Rosinger, L. B. Myers, G. W. Levy, M. Loar, S. Morhman, & J. R. Stock, "Development of a Behaviorally Based Performance Appraisal System," *Personnel Psychology*, Spring 1982, 75–88.

11. J. G. Goodale & M. W. Mouser, "Developing and Auditing a Merit Pay System," *Personnel Journal*, 60 (May 1981), 391–397.

12. G. S. Odiorne, *Management by Objectives: A System of Managerial Leadership.* (New York: Pitman, 1965);

    K. Albrecht, *Successful MBO: An Action Manual.* (New York: Prentice-Hall Press, 1988); and

    A. W. Schrader & G. T. Seward, "MBO Makes Dollar Sense," *Personnel Journal*, July 1989, 32–37.

13. H. H. Meyer, E. Kay, & J. P. R. French, Jr., "Split Roles in Performance Appraisal"; and

    L. Sandler, "Two-sided Performance Reviews," *Personnel Journal*, January 1990, 75–78.

14. N. R. F. Maier, *Psychology in Industrial Organizations*, 5th ed. (Boston: Houghton Mifflin, 1982).

15. Reprinted from N. R. F. Maier, *The Appraisal Interview* (New York: John Wiley & Sons, 1958), p. 22. Reprinted by permission of the publisher.

16. A. R. Karr, "Rating the Boss," *Wall Street Journal*, July 16, 1991, 1; and

    C. A. Norman and R. A. Zawacki, "Team Appraisals—Team Approach," *Personnel Journal*, September 1991, 101–104.

17. H. H. Meyer, "A Solution to the Performance Appraisal Feedback Enigma."

18. Adapted from N. R. F. Maier, *Psychology in Industrial Organizations*, pp. 578–581. Reprinted by permission of the publisher.

Chapter 4

1. P. C. Cairo, "Counseling in Industry: A Selected Review of the Literature," *Personnel Psychology*, Spring 1983, 1–18; and

   J. Greiff, "When an Employee's Performance Slumps," *Nation's Business*, 77 (January 1989), 44–45.

2. V. Pawlik & B. H. Kleiner, "On-the-Job Employee Counseling: Focus on Performance," *Personnel Journal*, 65 (November 1986), 31–36; and

   M. E. Cavanagh, "Employee Problems: Prevention and Intervention," *Personnel Journal*, September 1987, 35–40.

3. Rogers, C. R., *Counseling and Psychotherapy*. (Boston: Houghton Mifflin, 1951); and

   Ruch, W. A., "The Why and How of Nondirective Counseling," *Supervisory Management*, 18 (January 1973), 13–19.

4. T. J. Griffith, "Want Job Improvement? Try Counseling," *Management Solutions*, 32 (September 1987), 13–19;

   A. E. Schwartz, "Counseling the Marginal Performer," *Management Solutions*, 33 (March 1988), 30–35; and

   H. W. Smith, "Steps to Improved Performance Counselling," *Journal of Managerial Psychology*, 3 (1988), 3–7.

Chapter 5

1. "The End of Corporate Loyalty?" *Business Week*, August 4, 1986, 42–49.

2. D. T. Hall & Associates, *Career Development in Organizations*. (San Francisco: Jossey-Bass, 1986); and

   B. Moses & B. J. Chakiris, "The Manager as Career Counselor," *Training and Development Journal*, 43 (July 1989), 60–65.

3. D. T. Hall, *Careers in Organizations*. (Glenview, IL: Scott, Foresman, 1976).

4. B. Kaye, *Up Is Not the Only Way*. (Englewood Cliffs, NJ: Prentice-Hall, 1982); and

D. T. Hall & J. Richter, "Career Gridlock: Baby Boomers Hit the Wall," *The Executive*, 4 (August 1990), 7–22.

5. D. C. Miller & W. H. Form, *Industrial Sociology*. (New York: Harper, 1951);

   D. T. Hall & K. Nougaim, "An Examination of Maslow's Need Hierarchy in an Organizational Setting," *Organizational Behavior and Human Performance*, 3 (1968), 12–25;

   D. E. Super & M. J. Bohn, Jr., *Occupational Psychology*. (Belmont, CA: Wadsworth, 1970); and

   D. T. Hall, *Careers in Organizations*.

6. D. T. Hall & J. Richter, "Career Gridlock: Baby Boomers Hit the Wall."

7. D. T. Hall, *Careers in Organizations*.

8. B. Brophy, "You're Fired," *U.S. News & World Report*, March 23, 1987, 50–54;

   L. D. Foxman & W. L. Polsky, "How to Select a Good Outplacement Firm," *Personnel Journal*, 63 (September 1984), 94–97; and

   W. J. Morin & K. York, *Outplacement Techniques*. (New York: AMACOM, 1982).

9. D. T. Hall, *Careers in Organizations*, p. 201.

Chapter 6

1. All federal legislation cited in Chapter 2 applies also to discharging employees. In addition, state laws restrict employers' rights to lay off and discharge employees.

2. J. Stieber, "Employment-At-Will: An Issue for the 1980s," in R. S. Schuler, S. A. Youngblood, & V. L. Huber (eds) *Personnel and Human Resources Management*. (St. Paul: West Publishing, 1987), pp. 379–386.

3. A. W. Bryant, "Replacing Punitive Discipline with a Positive Approach," *Personnel Administrator*, February 1984, 79–87; and

   M. Levy, "Discipline for Professional Employees," *Personnel Journal*, December 1990, 27–28.

4. Reprinted by permission of Panhandle Eastern Corporation.

5. R. C. Grote, *Positive Discipline*. (New York: McGraw Hill, 1978); and

D. N. Campbell, R. L. Fleming, & R. C. Grote, "Discipline without Punishment—At Last," *Harvard Business Review*, 63 (July-August 1985), 162–178.

Index